Cool and Minty Christmas Cookie Wonders

Peppermint Perfection: Cool and Minty Holiday Delights

Nathan Mitchell

© Copyright 2023 - All rights reserved.

The content contained within this book may not be reproduced, duplicated or transmitted without direct written permission from the author or the publisher.

Under no circumstances will any blame or legal responsibility be held against the publisher, or author, for any damages, reparation, or monetary loss due to the information contained within this book, either directly or indirectly.

Legal Notice:

This book is copyright protected. It is only for personal use. You cannot amend, distribute, sell, use, quote or paraphrase any part, or the content within this book, without the consent of the author or publisher.

Disclaimer Notice:

Please note the information contained within this document is for educational and entertainment purposes only. All effort has been executed to present accurate, up to date, reliable, complete information. No warranties of any kind are declared or implied. Readers acknowledge that the author is not engaging in the rendering of legal, financial, medical or professional advice. The content within this book has been derived from various sources. Please consult a licensed professional before attempting any techniques outlined in this book. By

reading this document, the reader agrees that under no circumstances is the author responsible for any losses, direct or indirect, that are incurred as a result of the use of information contained within this document, including, but not limited to, errors, omissions, or inaccuracies.

Table of Contents

INTRODUCTION 6

CHAPTER I: The Allure of Peppermint 8

Exploring the timeless charm of peppermint during the holiday season 8

Historical significance and cultural traditions surrounding peppermint 11

How peppermint became a staple in Christmas treats........ 13

CHAPTER II: Essential Tools and Ingredients 18

A detailed list of tools needed for successful cookie baking 18

Key ingredients for creating cool and minty Christmas wonders 22

Tips and tricks for mastering the art of holiday baking 26

CHAPTER III: Classic Cool and Minty Cookies 32

Recipes for timeless favorites like Peppermint Bark Cookies and Mint Chocolate Chip Delights 32

Step-by-step instructions for perfecting these classic treats 35

Variations and creative twists to make each recipe unique. 39

CHAPTER IV: Innovative Minty Creations 43

Introducing modern and inventive cookie recipes with a minty twist 43

Unique flavor combinations and surprising ingredients...... 46

Showcasing how traditional recipes can be reinvented for a contemporary audience................................... 50

CHAPTER V: Gluten-Free and Vegan Options 54

Catering to dietary preferences with delicious gluten-free and vegan minty cookies 54

Tips on ingredient substitutions and maintaining flavor integrity 58

Generally speaking, while changing an ingredient, ... 61

Ensuring everyone can enjoy a cool and minty Christmas delight 62

CHAPTER VI: Decorative Techniques 66

Step-by-step guide to decorating cool and minty cookies 66

Using peppermint-themed designs and colors to enhance the festive spirit 69

Tips for creating visually stunning treats without compromising on taste 73

CHAPTER VII: Gift-Worthy Minty Packages 78

Ideas for packaging and presenting cool and minty Christmas cookies as gifts 78

DIY packaging options and creative presentation ideas.81

Tips for shipping cookies to loved ones near and far ... 85

CHAPTER VIII: Hosting a Minty Cookie Exchange 90

Planning and organizing a successful cool and minty cookie exchange party 90

Invitations, decorations, and activities to make the event memorable 93

Sharing the joy of holiday baking with friends and family 98

CHAPTER IX: Memories and Traditions 103

Reflecting on the role of cool and minty cookies in creating holiday memories 103

Collecting and preserving family recipes and traditions 107

Encouraging readers to create their own Christmas cookie traditions 111

CONCLUSION 116

Summing up the joy of baking cool and minty Christmas cookies 116

Encouraging readers to continue experimenting with flavors and creating new Traditions 119

Wishing everyone a season filled with Peppermint Perfectio 123

INTRODUCTION

"Welcome to the delectable world of Cool and Minty Christmas Cookie Wonders: Peppermint Perfection— a delightful section that infuses your holiday season with the sweet, refreshing magic of peppermint delights. In this festive collection, we invite you on a culinary journey through the enchanting realm of calm and minty holiday cookies that will tantalize your taste buds and add a touch of whimsy to your Christmas celebrations.

As you embark on this flavorful adventure, you'll discover a treasure trove of recipes meticulously curated to capture the essence of the holiday spirit. From classic peppermint bark cookies to innovative twists on traditional favorites, each recipe in this section is designed to transport you to a winter wonderland filled with the refreshing aroma of mint. Picture yourself savoring the perfect balance of sweetness and coolness in every bite as these cookies become the centerpiece of your festive gatherings.

The subtitle, 'Peppermint Perfection,' serves as a promise—each recipe within these virtual pages is a testament to the artistry of crafting the perfect cool and minty treat for your holiday table. Whether you're an experienced baker or a novice in the kitchen, the easy-to-follow instructions and helpful tips will empower you to create these delightful confections confidently.

Join us in embracing the season's spirit as we celebrate the joy of baking and sharing these Cool and Minty Christmas Cookie Wonders. May your holiday be filled with Peppermint Perfection, and may each cookie be a testament to the magic of Christmas and the joy of bringing loved ones together in sweet harmony."

CHAPTER I

The Allure of Peppermint

Exploring the timeless charm of peppermint during the holiday season

A diverse range of customs embellish the Christmas season, a period of festivity and shared delight, creating a vibrant tapestry of celebration. The everlasting fascination with Peppermint, which infuses our holiday customs with its cold, minty appeal, stands out among these treasured customs. With a rich cultural and culinary heritage, Peppermint is a seasonal favorite that brings back fond memories of coziness, warmth, and the wonder of the holidays.

Since ancient times, Peppermint has been associated with winter and used in many cultural customs. Because of the herb's inherent cooling qualities, it was a perfect fit for the Christmas season, blending well with the cozy warmth of holiday get-togethers and the crisp weather. Peppermint's flavor profile, which embodies the essence of the season in every refreshing mouthful, is an exquisite balance of sweetness and freshness that has come to be associated with the holiday spirit.

One of the most iconic peppermint-infused Christmas emblems is the candy cane, with its instantly recognizable red and white stripes that evoke fond memories. Beyond being visually pleasing, the candy cane has a deeper meaning; the crimson represents Christ's sacrifice and the white stands for purity. The candy cane, a beloved treat for kids and an ordinary ornament on Christmas trees has endured as a symbol of the joyous occasion.

That being said, Peppermint's appeal goes beyond the candy cane itself. A trend of chilly and minty Christmas goodies has emerged from the recent interest in incorporating peppermint flavors into various seasonal treats. Let me introduce you to the section "Cool and Minty Christmas Cookie Wonders: Peppermint Perfection," which takes readers on a culinary adventure exploring the art of creating delicious holiday cookies flavored with the revitalizing fragrance of Peppermint.

This section is a celebration of Peppermint's culinary inventiveness and adaptability. It goes beyond traditional applications and looks for creative ways to add this classic flavor to a range of cookie recipes. The section features a wide range of recipes to please both experienced bakers and culinary beginners, from traditional peppermint bark cookies that demonstrate the ideal combination of chocolate and mint to creative takes on time-honored favorites.

Beyond just its flavor, Peppermint is particularly appealing during the holidays because of its energizing scent, essential for establishing a festive mood. Peppermint is a popular aroma for scented candles, room sprays, and other holiday-themed fragrances because of its unique capacity to boost moods and create a sense of peace. Peppermint enhances the Christmas experience by transforming regular surroundings into winter wonderlands, whether used in baked delicacies or fragrant décor.

There's more to Peppermint than meets the eye; there's a psychological association with the holidays. In contrast to the rich and decadent flavors typically associated with holiday feasts, Peppermint's crisp and refreshing taste acts as a palate cleanser. Peppermint thus becomes a palate-cleansing interlude that resets taste buds and permits indulging in a wide range of holiday foods to the fullest.

During the holidays, Peppermint is famous in food and drinks and has become a staple flavor for unique occasion libations. Some ways this adaptable taste brings a little magic to the beverage scene in the winter are peppermint hot chocolate, candy cane coffee, and minty Christmas teas. These beverages' reassuring warmth and energizing peppermint kick combine to create a sensory experience that perfectly captures the season's essence.

Furthermore, Peppermint's alleged health advantages lend an additional degree of allure. Peppermint, well-known for its digestive qualities and capacity to calm upset stomachs, offers a cooling and nutritious substitute among the excesses of holiday feasting. In particular, peppermint tea has gained popularity as a soothing and help to digestion after a heavy holiday dinner.

In summary, Peppermint's perennial allure during the holiday season is a complex phenomenon beyond its flavor. Peppermint has become a staple of the holiday season, from its symbolic use in candy canes to its revival in modern culinary creations. During this unique time of year, Peppermint is a versatile and cherished ingredient due to its ability to elicit nostalgia, create a festive ambiance, and improve savory and sweet meals. As we delve into the world of "Cool and Minty Christmas Cookie Wonders: Peppermint Perfection," we celebrate the timeless magic of Peppermint, which has enchanted generations and continues to enchant holiday customs all over the world, in addition to indulging in the seasonal treats.

Historical significance and cultural traditions surrounding peppermint

With its revitalizing scent and excellent taste, peppermint has a long history and is essential to many cultural customs. Peppermint has been used since ancient times when its fragrant and therapeutic virtues made it highly prized. The herb is thought to have originated in Europe and is a hybrid of spearmint and watermint. Its origins are in ancient Egypt, where dried peppermint leaves were found in the pyramids, indicating that the Egyptians used it long ago for medical and culinary purposes.

Peppermint was a sign of hospitality in classical Greece and Rome and was used in many facets of daily life. While the Romans employed peppermint for its fragrant qualities in perfumes and bath oils, the Greeks used it as a flavoring agent in wines and dishes. During the Middle Ages, peppermint gained widespread renown throughout Europe, and because of its therapeutic properties, it was a mainstay in monastic gardens. Monks grew and used peppermint to treat respiratory, headache, and stomach ailments.
Peppermint's therapeutic benefits continued to garner attention during the Renaissance. It was widely grown in gardens and monasteries throughout Europe, and its essential oil rose to popularity. Due to its many uses, the plant was considered a significant asset in traditional medicine and was used to cure many diseases, including headaches and digestive difficulties. Because of

peppermint's long history as a therapeutic herb is now widely used in herbal medicine and apothecaries.

European settlers brought peppermint to the New World in the 18th century after realizing its culinary and therapeutic benefits. The herb flourished in the American environment and was swiftly included in American food and folk medicine. In particular, peppermint tea became well-known for its calming effects and delicious flavor. As peppermint was cultivated more widely, it became a commercial crop in the US.

Peppermint production became more industrialized in the 19th century when methods for extracting its essential oil through steam distillation were developed. This signaled a dramatic change in the methods for gathering and using peppermint. The pharmaceutical and confectionery industries adopted necessary oil as a crucial component, using it to make items like toothpaste, ointments, and peppermint candies.

Beyond its historical applications, peppermint has great cultural significance. It is now an essential component of holiday customs, especially in the winter. Candy canes and peppermint bark are two classic examples of peppermint-flavored delicacies associated with Christmas. The herb's incredible, refreshing flavor has come to be associated with joyous occasions, and its connection to the Christmas season has cemented its status in cultural customs.

Additionally, peppermint has been included in many other international culinary customs. It is a staple in many international cuisines, enhancing the taste of both savory and sweet meals. The herb peppermint has crossed cultural barriers to become a versatile culinary ingredient, appearing in everything from minty lamb dishes in the Middle East to desserts flavored with the herb in Europe.

Peppermint is used in traditional rites and rituals in addition to cooking. Peppermint is used to ward off evil spirits and offer good fortune in certain cultures. Its fragrant qualities are used in rituals to clean and purify areas. The plant is a common choice for rituals and ceremonies in many cultural contexts because of its associations with freshness and positive energy.

Peppermint has symbolic meaning even when its taste, aroma, and possible health advantages are appreciated. In aromatherapy, peppermint essential oil induces calmness and reduces tension. Because of the herb's cooling menthol component, it's frequently used as an ingredient in topical ointments and lotions for muscle relaxation and pain treatment.

In conclusion, peppermint's cultural customs and historical significance have influenced the herb's reputation as versatile and beloved. Peppermint has endured through the ages, from its ancient origins in Egypt and Greece to its extensive use in contemporary cuisine and medicine. To its already rich history, its connection to cultural customs and holiday celebrations has added a layer of symbolism. Peppermint is a herb with profound cultural and historical roots, and as its many uses are investigated, we discover that its appeal extends beyond taste and aroma.

How peppermint became a staple in Christmas treats

The transformation of peppermint from a therapeutic herb to a common ingredient in Christmas goodies is a fascinating story that weaves together history, culture, and the gastronomic pleasures associated with the holiday season. The connection between peppermint and

Christmas has deep roots that span ages and continents, producing a savory tradition that continues to fascinate our taste buds during the holiday season. Peppermint is a spice that is commonly used in Christmas cookies.

There is a connection between peppermint and Christmas that may be traced back to the historical significance of peppermint and its cultural use. Since ancient times, peppermint, a hybrid of spearmint and watermint, has been cultivated and valued for its refreshing flavor and aromatic features. The Egyptians were among the first to use it for culinary and medical purposes, which provided the groundwork for its widespread distribution across various cultures. Peppermint was included in a wide variety of products that were used daily in ancient Greece and Rome. These products included perfumes, bath oils, sauces, and wines. Peppermint was also considered a symbol of hospitality.

As the herb made its way across Europe during the Middle Ages, monks in monasteries began to embrace peppermint for its medical benefits. It quickly became a widespread cure for stomach difficulties, headaches, and respiratory concerns. During the Renaissance, peppermint cultivation expanded in European gardens and convent grounds, further solidifying its reputation as a medicinal herb. Peppermint has a long and illustrious history of use as a therapeutic and aromatic herb, which laid the groundwork for its eventual adoption into celebrations that are meant to be joyful.

In the 18th century, peppermint was carried to the New World, where it successfully established itself among European immigrants who realized its potential for use in culinary and medical applications. Because of the favorable climate in the United States, peppermint flourished, and its cultivation eventually increased, becoming a rich cash crop. An important turning point for peppermint occurred in the 19th century when industrialization brought about the introduction of steam distillation techniques for the extraction of its essential oil. This breakthrough resulted in the widespread usage of peppermint in the pharmaceutical and confectionery sectors, which laid the framework for peppermint's link with Christmas sweets.

During the 19th and early 20th centuries, the connection between peppermint and Christmas became more evident. The proliferation of candy manufacturing made it possible to produce peppermint-flavored goodies in large quantities, which was a step toward making them more available to the general population. This relationship is represented by the candy cane, which is a legendary symbol. There is a lot of controversy around the precise origin of the candy cane; however, it is generally accepted that the shape and flavor of the candy cane became connected with Christmas in the nineteenth century. Several hypotheses propose that the cane's shape represents a shepherd's crook, symbolizing the shepherds who would visit the infant Jesus. It is said that the red and white stripes symbolize the sacredness of Christ's blood and the cleanliness of humanity.
It didn't take long for peppermint candies and candy canes to become synonymous with holiday celebrations. Their flavor, which was sweet and minty, added a lovely touch to the celebrations that took place throughout the Christmas season, and they became highly popular as ornaments for Christmas trees. With time, the connection between peppermint and Christmas grew so profoundly in Western culture that it extended beyond the sphere of sweets. A sensory experience that

connects with the spirit of the Christmas season was created by peppermint-flavored pastries, beverages, and treats, which became classics during the holiday season.

The flavor of peppermint is not the only thing that makes it appealing during the Christmas season; it also carries with it a feeling of tradition and nostalgia. Many people relate the aroma and flavor of peppermint with fond memories of holiday get-togethers, meals with family, and decorations for the holiday season. Unwrapping a peppermint candy or biting into a delicacy with a peppermint taste produces a sensation of joy and warmth, which is why it is an essential component of the Christmas experience. Peppermint's cultural significance throughout Christmas goes beyond the United States and other Western countries. The herb is used to prepare traditional holiday dishes and sweets in several cultures. Peppermint is used to design unique Christmas bread, sweets, and beverages in several nations celebrating the holiday. The versatility and adaptability of peppermint are demonstrated by its widespread popularity throughout the Christmas season on a global scale. Peppermint can blend in effortlessly with a wide variety of culinary traditions.

In addition, the symbolism of peppermint is congruent with the concepts associated with Christmas. Its flavor, which is both refreshing and chilly, is reminiscent of the crispness of winter, and the association with purity and cleanliness is a perfect complement to the concept of beginning a new year with complete cleanliness. The fragrant properties of peppermint are utilized in the production of scented candles, oils, and decorations, producing a multisensory experience that contributes to enhancing the celebratory environment.

In recent years, there has been a steady increase in the acceptance of peppermint-flavored confections throughout the Christmas season. During the holiday season, there is a surge in demand for products that have a peppermint taste, including candies, pastries, and beverages (among other things). To capitalize on this trend, the food and beverage industries have introduced limited-edition peppermint offers that allow consumers the opportunity to satisfy their demands for festive foods. The fact that peppermint continues to be popular during the holiday season is evidence that it has the power to elicit feelings of joy and tradition.

In conclusion, the journey of peppermint from a simple herb with ancient medical uses to a mainstay in Christmas goodies is an intriguing story that threads through the fabric of human history and culture. Peppermint has been used for a variety of purposes throughout history. As a result of its refreshing flavor and fragrant properties, as well as its rich historical significance, it has become synonymous with joyous celebrations. Peppermint has become a symbol of Christmas joy, and it may be found in various forms, including candy canes, pastries, and beverages. It evokes a sensory experience that is resonant with history and nostalgia. At the same time that we are enjoying the unmistakable flavor of peppermint during the Christmas season, we are also participating in a cultural legacy that has been passed down for centuries and continues to enhance our celebrations with the essence of this cherished herb.

CHAPTER II

Essential Tools and Ingredients

A detailed list of tools needed for successful cookie baking

Baking cookies is an art that calls for accuracy, perseverance, and the correct instruments to guarantee the ideal texture, flavor, and look. Both aspiring and seasoned bakers know how important it is to have a well-stocked kitchen before starting the fun process of making mouthwatering cookies. A wide range of specialized utensils and essential measuring tools are critical for efficient cookie baking.

First and foremost, a trustworthy set of measuring equipment is essential to any baker's arsenal. The secret to every successful baking attempt is precise measurement. Precise amounts of components like flour, sugar, and cocoa powder can be made with a set of dry measuring cups, which have measurements ranging from 1/4 cup to 1 cup. Furthermore, liquid measuring cups with readable side markings help handle liquids like milk, oils, and vanilla extract. Different-sized measuring spoons guarantee precise proportions of tiny components like spices, baking soda, and powder. Purchasing high-quality measurement equipment is the first step toward consistently baking tasty cookies.

Another vital tool in the cookie baker's toolbox is a mixing bowl. Different stages of preparation, such as mixing wet and dry components or combining dry ingredients, are made possible by a range of sizes. Bowls made of glass, stainless steel, or heat-resistant plastic are frequently used, and each has benefits. Glass bowls make the ingredients easy to see, but stainless steel bowls are strong, odor-resistant, and stain- resistant. Plastic dishes that can withstand heat are perfect for jobs like microwave butter melting. Having a variety of mixing bowls guarantees efficiency and adaptability when preparing cookies.

Any cookie recipe's secret is mixing, and using a stand or hand mixer may change the game regarding getting the right consistency. A stand mixer, with many attachments like the paddle, whisk, and dough hook, is a strong and flexible instrument for larger quantities and a range of cookie recipes. In contrast, a hand mixer is more convenient and suitable for smaller batches. With the help of a dependable mixer, jobs like creaming butter and sugar, beating eggs, and kneading cookie dough become more accessible and add to the success of the baking endeavor.

A silicone and robust spatula are essential equipment for activities requiring a more delicate touch. A spatula helps fold delicate components; silicone spatulas are ideal for scraping bowls and ensuring no priceless cookie dough is lost due to their heat-resistant qualities. These adaptable tools may be used for various cookie recipes, from chewy chocolate chip cookies to delicate macarons.

Cookie cutters are the baker's equivalent of an artist's brush regarding cookie shapes and sizes. With so many different cookie cutters available, there are countless ways to create imaginative shapes for kids or festive holiday sweets. Cookie cutters allow bakers to express their creativity and personalize their delicious creations with various designs, from simple circles to more complex patterns. Purchasing cookie stamps or embossing tools add a decorative aspect that transforms plain cookies into delectable art pieces.

Rolling pins are needed to roll cookie dough to a consistent thickness. Whether fashioned of marble, wood, or stainless steel, a high-quality rolling pin guarantees even and seamless results. It is an essential tool for any dough recipe for rolling and cutting into exact shapes, such as sugar cookies or gingerbread. To further streamline the baking process, some rolling pins even have movable rings to keep a constant thickness. An oven thermometer is a modest but essential equipment for reaching the right temperature in the oven. Accuracy in the oven is critical to the success of cookies. Oven accuracy varies, so bakers can make required modifications to guarantee equal baking based on the accurate reading that an oven thermometer offers. Maintaining a constant temperature is essential for producing cookies with a crisp, golden brown outside and a soft, perfectly baked inside.

Parchment section or silicone baking mats are necessary to keep cookies from sticking to baking sheets. Providing a non-stick surface, parchment section is adaptable for various baking applications. Conversely, silicone baking mats are both eco-friendly and reusable. They result in precisely shaped and baked goodies by promoting equal heat distribution and preventing cookies from spreading too much.

A sturdy pair of cookie sheets or baking pans guarantees that cookies bake uniformly and have the right texture. These tools are essential to the baking process. While expert bakers often prefer insulated cookie sheets to avoid uneven browning, non-stick ones are still popular.

The sort of cookie being cooked determines which pan is best, and having a range of sizes and kinds in the kitchen makes cooking more versatile.

Cooling racks are the last step in baking, used once the cookies are perfectly baked. Ensuring that air circulates hot cookies when placed immediately onto a cooling rack helps to reduce sogginess and promote even cooling. Cooling racks, whether wire or stainless steel, are an easy-to-use but essential tool for getting the perfect texture in cookies.

A cookie scoop comes in various sizes to portion cookie batter onto baking sheets. This guarantees consistency in size, making for uniformly baked and aesthetically pleasing cookies. When working with sticky or thick cookie dough, cookie scoops are helpful because they reduce mess and expedite the baking process.

Pipette bags and decorative tips become indispensable equipment for cookie decorators wanting to step it up. These make creating elaborate patterns, embellishments, and motifs possible, mainly when using royal icing or other ornamental accents. Piping bags offer versatility depending on the baker's preference and the size of the baking endeavor. They are available in disposable or reusable varieties.

A digital kitchen scale is a valuable tool for baking cookies that is frequently disregarded. Accuracy is ensured when ingredients are measured by weight instead of volume, especially in recipes that need precision—a kitchen scale benefits bakers who wish to repeat successful recipes and attain consistent results confidently.

When enhancing flavor, a zester or microplane grater gives cookie recipes a zesty or spicy kick. Zest from lemons, oranges, or freshly grated nutmeg are some ingredients that add richness to cookie flavors. A dash of zest may turn an ordinary sugar cookie into something special or give a chocolate chip recipe a novel touch.

Finally, just as significantly, baking possibilities are increased with high-quality bakeware, such as cake pans, muffin tins, and specialty molds. Even though cookies are typically baked on sheets, bakers can experiment with different shapes and sizes by having a variety of bakeware. Whoopie pies, bar cookies, and miniature muffin tin cookies demonstrate how adaptable cookie recipes can be when used with the appropriate baking tools.

To sum up, baking cookies successfully is an art that calls for a diverse toolkit. From precise measuring tools to multipurpose mixing equipment, shaping tools, and oven-safe precision instruments, every item is essential to turning raw ingredients into delicious cookies. Both novices and seasoned baking enthusiasts understand the value of purchasing high-quality equipment since it enhances the enjoyment and fulfillment of baking and the success of specific recipes. The appropriate equipment makes baking fun and fulfilling, whether making traditional chocolate chip cookies or more complex seasonal delights. Plus, they leave a trail of tasty cookies in their wake.

Key ingredients for creating cool and minty Christmas wonders

Making cold, minty delights for the holidays is a magical culinary journey that starts with a well-chosen list of essential ingredients. The combination of refreshing mint and coolness transports one to the mood of winter and holiday parties while providing a taste experience beyond conventional pairings. These essential components—the adaptable peppermint and complimentary tastes and textures—help create delicious confections that become symbols of the holiday season.

The distinct flavor of peppermint is the foundation of many cold and minty Christmas delights. Peppermint is a perennial herb with deep historical value, a cross between spearmint and watermint. It's also a staple in Christmas confections. Peppermint is an excellent ingredient for desserts and drinks with a Christmas theme because of its crisp, refreshing flavor that goes well with the wintertime decor. This necessary component is concentrated in peppermint extract from the peppermint plant's leaves. A tiny peppermint essence adds minty deliciousness, turning an otherwise plain meal into a Christmas feast.

Candy canes and peppermint candies are the ultimate Christmas miracles. These classic candies, which dress up Christmas trees and add a hint of sweetness to stockings, are a symbol of the festive season. Candy peppermints, striped, twisted, or fashioned like canes, provide a lovely touch for sweets and drinks. When candy canes are crushed and added to dishes, like peppermint bark or cookies, they add a delicious crunch that improves the flavor and texture of the dish.

In the world of chilly, minty Christmas delights, chocolate and peppermint make a dynamic combination that has become a classic. The chill of peppermint and the richness of chocolate combine to create a perfect blend that is both decadent and celebratory. A favorite Christmas delicacy, peppermint bark combines crushed peppermint candies with white or dark chocolate to create a treat that perfectly embodies the season's spirit. In addition, chocolate and peppermint combine to create a symphony of flavors in cookies, brownies, and hot cocoa that convey warmth and comfort amid winter's chill.

Christmas miracles gain a delicious crunch and nutty flavor from the inclusion of crushed almonds, which goes beyond the classic coupling of chocolate and peppermint. Toasted pecans, almonds, or walnuts add a pleasing texture that plays well against the smoothness of chocolate or the softness of baked products when mixed with excellent minty flavors. Holiday desserts with nut-studded peppermint fudge or cookies provide another level of complexity and appeal to people who love a blend of creamy, crunchy, and minty flavors. Mint-infused syrups and extracts are essential in refreshing, minty drinks. Some beverages that embody the season perfectly are candy cane martinis, mint hot chocolate, and peppermint mochas. Made by simmering sugar, water, and fresh mint leaves, mint-infused simple syrup gives coffee, hot cocoa, and cocktails a flavor boost. Because mint-infused syrups are so versatile, mixologists may get creative with their concoctions and create signature drinks that perfectly capture Christmas's crisp, minty vibe.

Beyond baked foods and drinks, cool and minty marvels include frozen sweets that add a cool edge to Christmas festivities. With its swirls of chocolate flakes or crushed candy canes, peppermint ice cream offers a refreshing break from the wintertime celebrations. Peppermint sorbet, presented in classy bowls or as a palette cleanser between courses, demonstrates how invigorating and refreshing the herb can be. Frosted minty beauties bring a whimsical and surprising aspect to Christmas get-togethers, leaving a lasting impression on those who indulge in these icy treats.

Add fresh herbs like spearmint or mint to dishes to enhance the relaxed, minty feel. Finely chopped or garnished with fresh mint leaves, these add a natural mint flavor and visual appeal to desserts and drinks. A visually pleasing and aesthetically pleasing finishing touch can be applied to cookies by dusting them with mint sugar or making whipped cream with mint flavor. Adding fresh herbs enhances the freshness of chilly, minty Christmas delights, resulting in a multisensory delight that perfectly captures the season's essence. A sophisticated twist is provided by including peppermint liqueurs and spirits for those looking for a more grown-up, chilled, and minty experience. Classic holiday delicacies can be made into adult-friendly cocktails, including peppermint schnapps, crème de menthe, or peppermint-infused vodka. These spirits can be used to create a variety of sophisticated and comforting drinks, such as peppermint martinis, spiked hot chocolate, and minty mojitos, which enhance celebrations.

Regarding baked foods, the cold, minty marvels are included in various cookie variants. With every bite, peppermint thumbprint cookies—a well pushed into the middle filled with peppermint ganache—offer a pleasant surprise. For people who enjoy rich, flavorful foods, chocolate peppermint sandwich cookies are a delectable treat with a creamy mint filling sandwiched between two chocolate cookies. With chilly and minty variants of traditional cookie recipes that suit a wide variety of palates, the options are virtually limitless.

To sum up, making cold and minty Christmas miracles requires a thoughtful combination of essential ingredients to capture the season's essence. Every ingredient has a unique effect on the sensory experience of holiday sweets, from the classic peppermint candy and vital peppermint essence to the taste combination of chocolate and almonds. Fresh herb infusions, sophisticated peppermint liqueurs, and inventive frozen treats combine to create a wide range of refreshing, minty treats that entice the senses and leave a lasting

impression. These essential components are used to create dishes that satisfy cravings and capture the spirit and wonder of Christmas as the holiday season progresses.

Tips and tricks for mastering the art of holiday baking

Learning to bake for the holidays is a fun project that makes parties happier and cozier. The smell of spices, the taste of baked products, and the excitement of sharing delectable delights with loved ones fill the kitchen as the season progresses, turning it into a center of activity. Whether you're an experienced baker or a beginner, following a few pointers will take your holiday baking to a new level and guarantee that your products are aesthetically pleasing and incredibly tasty.

Careful preparation is one of the critical components of a successful holiday baking endeavor. Ensure you have all the ingredients on hand, check your recipes, and make a shopping list before you get caught up in the tornado of flour and sugar. Think about the required tools, and make sure everything is sanitized and operational. By preparing beforehand, you can easily handle baking, reducing tension and enhancing the pleasure of making holiday goodies.

An essential component of good baking is realizing the significance of precise measures. The accuracy of components can make a big difference in the outcome, particularly in recipes with complex flavor profiles. Invest in sturdy measuring equipment, such as spoons and liquid and dry measuring cups. To ensure that your baked items have the right texture, avoid compressing flour into the measuring cup when measuring dry ingredients like flour. Instead, use the spoon-and-level approach.

Maintaining a precise temperature is essential for producing consistently tasty results. Before using any ingredients in your recipes, ensure they are at room temperature, especially butter and eggs. Ingredients that are too cold may not properly emulsify and produce uneven textures. In a similar vein, even baking requires preheating your oven. You may be sure that your items will bake as planned by using an oven thermometer to check the accuracy of your oven temperature.

Pick fresh and high-quality ingredients when choosing your ingredients. The quality of your ingredients directly influences the taste and texture of your baked items. Make an investment in premium chocolate, fresh eggs, extracts, spices, and butter. Your Christmas goodies will stand out and leave a lasting impact on people who enjoy them because of the enhanced taste and aroma of using fresh ingredients.

Experimenting with tastes is a great approach to add some originality to your holiday baking. Though we have a soft spot for classic dishes, feel free to add your spin using unusual tastes. For complexity, try experimenting with citrus zests, cardamom ginger spices, or a hint of espresso. The holidays are a time to savor flavor; being creative can provide a unique and unforgettable dining experience.

Your Christmas baking takes on a festive feel when you use seasonal ingredients. A few ingredients that can give your delights a pop of color and seasonal taste include fresh cranberries, pomegranate seeds, and citrus fruits. To convey the warmth and coziness of the season, try adding spices like cloves, nutmeg, and cinnamon. Using seasonal ingredients improves the appearance of your baked products and ties them into the holiday atmosphere.

The enjoyment of baked goods largely depends on texture, and obtaining the ideal consistency demands meticulous attention to detail. When adding flour, pay great attention to the timing and technique of mixing. Overmixing can cause a texture to become more rigid, especially in cakes and biscuits. On the other hand, undermixing may result in flour pockets that alter the consistency as a whole. You may perfect the art of getting the ideal crumb in your Christmas goodies by knowing the proper texture for each recipe.

Patience is a critical component of a good holiday baking recipe. Let your dough rest. Your cookies should cool on the baking sheet before moving them to a cooling rack, and your cakes should cool completely before frosting. Every stage of the baking process requires patience, which adds to the final product's success. Compromising textures and looks might result from icing warm cakes too quickly or rushing the cooling process. Accept the flow of the baking process and let each step happen at its speed.

Rolling dough to a consistent thickness might be challenging, especially for recipes calling for pie crusts or cut-out cookies. Use silicone rolling pin rings or cruising pin guides to ensure uniform thickness. These tools guarantee that your dough is moved to the proper thickness, which leads to beautifully formed and uniformly baked delights. Your Christmas crafts will look better if you take the time to measure and roll out your dough precisely.

Your holiday goodies will have an additional layer of charm if you embrace the art of decorating. Decorating is a creative outlet; it can create detailed designs on gingerbread houses, gracefully piped frosting on biscuits, or a coating of powdered sugar on cakes. To make your ideas come to life, spend money on high-quality decorating supplies like food coloring, tips, and piping bags. Try new methods, such as covering cookies in royal icing or decorating cakes with textured designs. Decorating is a great way to add a unique touch and capture the spirit of the occasion to your baked goods.

Applying mise en place, French for "everything in its place," is a skilled chef's method to improve your holiday baking significantly. Assemble and arrange all of your supplies and ingredients before you begin baking. Chop any nuts or fruits, measure out your wet and dry ingredients, and get ready any parts that need to be built. Everything is accessible and arranged, making baking easier and freeing you up to concentrate on the artistic creation of mouthwatering holiday goodies.

While accuracy is essential during baking, flexibility is also beneficial, mainly when unforeseen difficulties occur. If you discover that an ingredient is missing, look into possible replacements. For instance, buttermilk can frequently be swapped out for sour cream or vice versa. Knowing each ingredient's function in a recipe helps you make wise choices when needed. The delight of baking for the holidays is preserved even in minor setbacks when one is adaptable enough to change with the circumstances.

Cleaning as you go is a technique that improves productivity and increases baking enjoyment. As you work through your recipes, take care of the dishes rather than leaving them until the conclusion of your baking session. This keeps your workspace tidy and frees you from the distraction of a messy kitchen so you can concentrate on your creative process. Keeping the kitchen neat and organized makes baking during the holidays more enjoyable and creates the ideal environment for a flawless culinary journey.

Anyone serious about becoming an expert at holiday baking should consider investing in high-quality bakeware. Even baking and reliable outcomes are facilitated by using high-quality baking pans, cookie sheets, and molds. When choosing bakeware, things like non-stick surfaces, sturdy construction, and appropriate dimensions should all be considered. Purchasing top-notch equipment guarantees that your creations are baked to perfection, enabling you to be proud of the flavor and appearance of your festive confections.

The last and most important piece of advice for perfecting the art of Christmas baking is to embrace a spirit of creativity and joy. The holidays are a time to cherish customs, make new ones, and spread the cheer of delectable delicacies to those you care about. Feel free to experiment with different dishes, let your imagination run wild, and enjoy realizing your culinary dreams. Baking is more than just the finished product—it's about the happiness of making something unique for those you love.

Mastering the art of holiday baking requires a little creativity mixed with meticulous planning, exact measurement, and attention to detail. Choosing premium ingredients and embracing the tastes and textures of the season, each

Each step helps to create sweets that are both delicious and visually appealing. The secret is approaching the process with patience, adaptability, and a sincere appreciation for baking, whether creating traditional recipes or experimenting with new flavors. May the season's joy permeate every ingredient, measurement, and step as you embark on your holiday baking excursions, producing a symphony of tastes that provides warmth and delight to those fortunate enough to enjoy your festive creations.

CHAPTER III

Classic Cool and Minty Cookies

Recipes for timeless favorites like Peppermint Bark Cookies and Mint Chocolate Chip Delights

The act of indulging in the pleasures of holiday baking frequently entails the creation of classic favorites that recall the spirit of the season. Peppermint Bark Cookies and Mint Chocolate Chip Delights are two examples of such cherished sweets that have become linked with joyous occasions and celebrations because of their popularity. These dishes, each featuring a distinctive blend of flavors and textures, provide a delicious way to include the refreshing and minty sensation of the holiday
season in your culinary creations.

A delicious take on the traditional sugar cookie, Peppermint Bark Cookies captures the spirit of winter with a perfect combination of sweetness and cold mint. These cookies are a delightful twist on cookies. Take the first step in embarking on this culinary journey by beginning with a simple sugar cookie dough sweetened with a dab of vanilla essence. The dough should be rolled out into rounds and baked until the edges become golden brown. What makes these cookies stand out from others is the enticing peppermint bark that is sprinkled on top. The bark is made by melting high-quality white chocolate and blending it with peppermint extract, which imparts a flavor that is unmistakably bitter and refreshing. Spread the white chocolate mixture generously over the sugar cookies and allow them to cool, producing a silky smooth and delectable base.

The following layer features a striking contrast of dark chocolate, which is fun. A decadent dark chocolate should be melted, and then it should be drizzled over the cookies that have been covered in white chocolate. Not only does this procedure improve the aesthetic appeal, but it also brings about a beautiful symphony of sweet and bitter undertones. Peppermint candy canes or peppermint candies that have been crushed and sprinkled over the chocolate layers will finish the masterpiece perfectly. The result is a beautiful combination of textures, with the sugar cookie having a crisp texture, the white and dark chocolate having a smooth feel, and the peppermint having a pleasing crunch. The Peppermint Bark Cookies, once they have been allowed to set, transform into an enticing dessert that perfectly captures the enchantment of the Christmas season.

Mint Chocolate Chip Cookies are a perennial favorite among those who enjoy calm and minty treats. These cookies combine chocolate's decadence with peppermint's revitalizing flavor, making them a perfect combination of the two flavors. This recipe takes the traditional chocolate chip cookie into a culinary beauty perfect for the holiday season. Start by making a chocolate chip cookie dough fortified with peppermint extract. Peppermint extract is an essential component that gives the cookies a refreshing flavor reminiscent of mint. To ensure every bite is graced with velvety pools of chocolate, you should fold in high-quality chocolate chunks or chips.

The tempting scent of chocolate and mint permeates the house as the cookies bake to golden perfection before

being removed from the oven. The result is a batch of cookies with the ideal combination of chewiness and crispness, with beautifully golden edges and wonderfully soft cores. Consider adding a sprinkling of finely chopped fresh mint leaves to the dough or garnishing the baked cookies with a dusting of powdered sugar infused with mint to accentuate the minty allure. Because of the contrast between the dark chocolate and the light crumb, these Mint Chocolate Chip Cookies are a visual treat and a harmonious ballet of tastes that
captivates the taste buds with each mouthful.

One thing that both Peppermint Bark Cookies and Mint Chocolate Chip Delights have in common is the peppermint flavor. Due to its refreshing and invigorating profile, Peppermint emerges as the star of these recipes, imbuing the sweets with a festive allure reminiscent of the customs associated with the holiday season. The flexibility of peppermint extends beyond its flavor; it also contributes to the visual appeal of these products. One example is the Peppermint Bark Cookies, which have a festive touch thanks to crushed candy canes' brilliant red and white hues.

These recipes are magical not only because of the individual components but also because they combine to produce an experience that engages several senses. Whether it be a sugar cookie or chocolate chip basis, the base's texture is a canvas for the silky chocolate layers and the peppermint crunch. Meanwhile, the perfume of mint wafts through the air, taking anybody in the base's area to the fascinating world of holiday baking.
The quality of the ingredients is the driving force behind the success of any dish that has stood the test of time. In the case of Mint Chocolate Chip Cookies, a memorable indulgence can be created by selecting

chocolate of superior quality, fresh peppermint essence, and premium chocolate chips. This will ensure the tastes can show through and provide a memorable experience. The recipes provided here allow you to demonstrate your culinary expertise and spread the season's joy to your loved ones and friends.

These Christmas delights are genuinely ageless since they have the power to elicit feelings of nostalgia while at the same time providing an experience that is both new and thrilling. The Peppermint Bark Cookies and the Mint Chocolate Chip Delights are not only sweets; they are delicious manifestations of the spirit of the Christmas season. It is a chance to connect with cherished traditions and make new memories with loved ones; all made possible via creating these delicacies, which become a joyful ritual.

Consider the happiness and coziness that Peppermint Bark Cookies and Mint Chocolate Chip Delights offer as you embark on the road of holiday baking. It doesn't matter if you're baking for a holiday get-together, a cookie exchange, or to relish the delights of the season; these recipes are likely to become treasured classics in your collection of recipes. These holiday goodies are a marvelous invitation to celebrate the magic of baking and the joy of sharing exquisite creations with those you hold dear. With their classic charm and the enchantment of peppermint, these treats are a delicious invitation.

Step-by-step instructions for perfecting these classic treats

A pleasure that is eternal and transcends generations is the act of indulging in traditional sweets. The flaky layers of a well-cooked croissant and the rich, gooey texture of a chocolate chip cookie are just two examples of how these well-loved treats can bring warmth and happiness. However, to perfect these classics, you need more than just a little bit of expertise; you need precision, patience, and a bit of culinary grace. In this section, we will go into detailed directions for reaching perfection in two sweet delights among the most iconic: chocolate chip cookies and croissants.

Let's start with the skill of making the ideal croissant, a type of pastry that was first created in France and has since become a standard item in bakeries worldwide. One of the most important aspects of a perfect croissant is striking a precise balance between the layers of buttery sweetness and the light and airy interior. Mix high-quality flour, sugar, salt, yeast, and warm milk to prepare the dough. This will be the first step in the process. The dough should rest and rise to give the yeast sufficient time to perform its magic.

The next essential step is to laminate the dough with butter, which is a technique that requires the dough to be folded and rolled several times. In this case, the objective is to produce discrete layers divided by a thin butter sheet. It is precisely this methodical stacking that is responsible for the flakiness that is characteristic of croissants. To accomplish this, please ensure the butter is kept cool and malleable but could be more firm. When it comes to this phase, precision is of the utmost importance; a dough that has been appropriately laminated will result in a pastry that breaks apart with each bite.

After the lamination process, the dough should be sliced into triangles, and each triangle should be rolled out into the traditional crescent shape. A proofing period should be allowed for the shaped croissants until they have doubled in size. This stage is essential for the development of flavor and texture. After everything is said and done, bake the croissants until they reach golden perfection and appreciate the anticipation of the delicious aroma that will fill the house.

Now that we have shifted our attention to sweet treats let's investigate the procedure of baking the ideal chocolate chip cookies step by step. Because of their tender interiors, crisp edges, and the irresistible combination of cookie dough and melted chocolate, these delectable delights have stood the test of time and remain a fan favorite. To achieve this level of perfection, it is necessary to have a solid understanding of the science of cookie baking.

Initially, begin by combining butter and sugars at room temperature and creaming them together until the mixture becomes frothy and light. Performing this process ensures that the cookies have the perfect texture, which is soft and chewy on the inside and has a slight crunch on the outside. Add the eggs one at a time and wait until each is completely incorporated into the mixture before adding the next one. This slow addition guarantees that the batter will be smooth and consistent throughout.

The dry ingredients, including flour, baking soda, and salt, should be mixed in a separate basin. It is necessary to sift these ingredients together to remove any lumps and to guarantee that the leavening agents are distributed evenly. Mix the dry ingredients into the wet mixture slowly and steadily until they are completely incorporated. Excessive mixing might make cookies challenging to chew; therefore, resisting the urge to overmix is essential.

Without a doubt, the chocolate is the most essential part of the presentation. When making the cookie dough, use chocolate chunks or chips of good quality by folding them in. Making sure that the chocolate is evenly distributed throughout the dough is necessary to get a chocolate-to-cookie ratio that is both balanced and enjoyable. Another essential step is to chill the dough, which improves the flavor and stops the cookies from spreading too much when baked through the baking process.

When it is time to bake, divide the dough into portions and place them on a baking sheet prepared with parchment section. Make sure to leave enough room between each cookie to allow for spreading. The ideal cookie should have a golden brown surface and a middle that is just slightly undercooked. Paying close attention to the baking periods and temperatures is necessary to achieve this equilibrium.

Mastering the classics, whether it be chocolate chip cookies or croissants, needs more than technical talent; it also involves a grasp of the materials, an appreciation for the artistry of baking, and an understanding of the processes involved. When it comes to the world of pastry, patience is a virtue, and the ability to embrace the defects that give each treat its own identity is also significant.

In conclusion, whether you find comfort in the buttery layers of a croissant or the comforting sweetness of a chocolate chip cookie, the road of refining these classics is one that you should not hesitate to undertake. The satisfaction of making these sweets with your hands, appreciating the aroma as they bake, and savoring the first mouthwatering bite is a reward that cannot be compared to anything else. Prepare yourself for the culinary journey of mastering these classic delicacies by rolling up your sleeves, preheating the oven, and getting ready to embark on this quest. Your taste buds will be grateful to you for the effort, and the delight of making something great from scratch will remain with you long after the last crumbs have been wiped away.

Variations and creative twists to make each recipe unique

Creativity in the culinary arts frequently results from a willingness to test the limits of acceptable practices. Recipes that have been around for a long time serve as a basis, a canvas on which both professional chefs and home cooks can weave their unique originality. Within the scope of this section, we investigate the art of culinary reinvention using modifications and creative twists, with a particular emphasis on two universally cherished classics: the adaptable pasta dish and the everlasting apple pie.

As a culinary cornerstone deeply established in Italian cuisine, pasta provides a blank canvas for exploring different culinary techniques. The typical spaghetti dish with marinara sauce has been a mainstay for a long time, yet the possibilities for customization are as limitless as one's imagination may be. To illustrate, consider the art of making a velvety Alfredo sauce that lavishly coats fettuccine noodles. The recipe can be elevated even further by including grilled chicken, sun-dried tomatoes, and a hint of fresh basil. This will result in a masterpiece that the Mediterranean inspires.

Variants of pasta that are influenced by Asian cuisine create a confluence of flavors that fascinate the taste senses. These variants go beyond the traditions of Italian cuisine. Imagine a bowl of noodles with sesame and ginger, garnished with vibrant veggies and juicy shrimp, combining the finest Italian and Asian culinary worlds. The dynamic potential for reimagining traditional pasta dishes is demonstrated by this meal, which transcends the commonplace with its play of textures and exotic smells.

As we transfer our attention to the realm of sweets, the world-famous apple pie takes the spotlight as the show's star. This time-honored dessert is given a fresh lease on life through inventive reinterpretations even though the traditional version, with its flaky crust and apple filling that has been kissed with cinnamon, has a special place in the hearts of culinary enthusiasts. Imagine an apple pie with a drizzle of caramel on top, which provides a delicious contrast of sweetness against the sourness of the apples. To improve the flavor profile and give a sophisticated twist that satisfies the senses, sprinkle a hint of sea salt on top of the dish.

By drawing influence from cuisines from around the world, a spiced apple pie infused with chai tastes provides a taste experience reminiscent of the bustling streets of India. A warming and fragrant sensation can be achieved by investing the apple filling with chai spices, such as cardamom, cinnamon, and ginger. A fusion dessert is created when classic American apple pie and Indian chai spices are combined. This delicacy is a tribute to the many different culinary traditions that have influenced it.

From the selection of ingredients to the very form of the meal itself, reinventing classics encompasses a wide range of approaches. It would help if you considered transforming the traditional lasagna, often stacked in layers to achieve perfection, into a roll-up version of the playful and visually spectacular dish. Roll the lasagna noodles into individual servings, fill them with a mixture of ricotta and spinach, and bake them until they reach the desired level of golden perfection. The end product is a dish that presents a creative and sophisticated spin on a classic dish while retaining the essence of the traditional dish.

It is possible to reinterpret the modest apple pie as individual hand pies, a dessert option that can be considered. The spirit of a traditional pie is captured in these portable delicacies, featuring the contemporary convenience of taking and going. The individual portions allow experimenting with various crusts, fillings, and even dipping sauces, enabling a personalized touch that adds flair to something already known.
In addition to making structural adjustments and substituting ingredients, the skill of flavor pairing is an essential component in reinventing classic dishes. Take, for example, a pasta meal that features truffle oil and wild mushrooms, which are unexpected additions to the dish's flavor profile. Combining the earthy richness of truffle oil with the umami notes of mushrooms, a straightforward pasta meal may be elevated to a gourmet experience that titillates the taste senses.

Similarly, an apple pie can be made more complicated by incorporating unorthodox components like balsamic vinegar and black pepper into the recipe. The sweetness of the apples is complemented by the acidic depth of the balsamic vinegar, and a touch of black pepper gives a slight kick to the dish. By demonstrating the possibilities for creativity in the kitchen, this bold taste combination challenges conventional assumptions of what an apple pie may be and reflects the opportunity for innovation.

The utilization of alternate grains and flours has the potential to considerably broaden the scope of possibilities for reimagining traditional dishes. You can make a lighter, gluten-free alternative to typical wheat pasta by substituting zucchini noodles. This will provide a refreshing variation to a dish traditionally made with wheat pasta. When it comes to apple pie, experimenting with a crust based on nuts, such as almond or hazelnut flour, includes introducing a new layer of flavor and texture that matches the sweetness of the filling.

The secret of practical reinvention resides in the perfect marriage of flavors and textures, even though these modifications and creative tweaks bring a contemporary flair to existing classics. It is essential that a clever variation not overshadow the fundamental components that make a dish a classic but rather enhances them. Finding the optimal equilibrium demands a sophisticated grasp of the elements that make up a dish and an intuitive sense of how those components interact to produce a coherent and enjoyable culinary experience. The dynamic interplay between innovation and tradition is the driving force behind the success of the culinary arts sector. Classic recipes are given a new lease on life by applying unique twists and variations, providing a canvas for individual expression and discovering culinary experiences. These options are as boundless as the imagination of those wielding the spatula. The choices are practically endless, whether the reassuring embrace of an artistically recreated spaghetti dish or the delicious nostalgia of an apple pie with a modern twist. The kitchen should be a playground where classics are turned into something distinctly yours, and you should embrace the voyage of reinvention known as the culinary journey.

CHAPTER IV

Innovative Minty Creations

Introducing modern and inventive cookie recipes with a minty twist

Within the baking community, cookies are a classic example of the pure happiness that can be achieved with the right combination of flour, sugar, and butter. But ingenuity and inventiveness give the known fresh life, and how better to improve the traditional cookie than by adding a cool, minty twist? In this section, we take a culinary voyage, presenting creative and contemporary cookie recipes that honor history while tantalizing the palate with minty freshness.

Although the traditional chocolate chip cookie has long been a family favorite, adding peppermint essence creates a fun and surprising twist. Imagine the union of excellent, refreshing peppermint essence with decadent, dark chocolate chips—a symphony of flavors that elevates the ordinary to the extraordinary. A delightful crunch and a delightful infusion of mint are added by finely crushed candy canes, making each mouthful of this biscuit a joyful celebration.

A contemporary contender for cookie lovers is a mint chocolate sandwich cookie, which gets its name from the iconic Girl Scout Thin Mints. Indulgence is redefined by the marriage of rich chocolate covering, perfectly minted buttercream, and soft chocolate cookies. These sandwich cookies please the tastes of those looking for a more refined cookie experience while paying attention to tradition with their ideal combination of sweetness and minty freshness.

Moving outside of the chocolate box, imagine adding mint to a buttery shortbread treat. Combining the refreshing burst of peppermint with the crunchy, melt-in-your-mouth shortbread makes for a sophisticated yet approachable biscuit. When dipped in rich dark chocolate, these minty shortbread treats add a layer of richness, turning them from a basic biscuit to a gourmet treat for any occasion.

When mint is added, the traditional sugar cookie— already a blank canvas for artistic interpretation— becomes a vivid and revitalizing masterpiece. With a bright green hue, peppermint extract is added to the cookie dough, giving the cookies a festive, minty flavor and colorful pop of color. With their thin covering of mint-flavored royal icing and sprinkling of crushed candy canes, these minty sugar cookies perfectly encapsulate the spirit of the holidays.

A ginger-mint snap cookie is an excellent choice for individuals who want one that combines the warmth of spices with the refreshing taste of mint. Adding peppermint essence elevates the classic snap of a ginger cookie, making it a peppery and revitalizing treat. These cookies appeal visually to any cookie selection when rolled in sugar before baking and shimmering with a delicate frost.

As we explore the realm of creative cookie recipes, mint is more than just extracts and oils. A more complex and herbal version of the traditional minty cookie may be found in the mint-infused chocolate chunks made by steeping fresh mint leaves in heated cream before incorporating them into the cookie dough. Real mint leaves are infused into the cookie to provide a sophisticated and understated flavor and a visual element with bits of green scattered throughout.

The world of herbs offers new ideas for creative cookies beyond the classic mint. Adding basil to a lemon-basil shortbread cookie produces an unexpected and pleasant contrast with its sweet and somewhat spicy aromas. The citrus sharpness of the lemon and the herbaceous nuances of the basil combine to create a refined and refreshing cookie, a taste adventure that delights the palate.

Experimenting with textures is as crucial as flavorings to create creative mint-infused cookies. Imagine a deep, fudgy texture combined with the ideal ratio of cocoa to mint in a chewy chocolate cookie. This deviation from the typical crispness of many cookies adds a luxurious layer, making for a delightfully tough and revitalizing minty cookie.

Regarding creative minty sweets, "stuffed" cookies are paramount. Picture a double chocolate cookie stuffed to the brim with a cream filling that tastes like mint, much like a traditional Oreo. The contrast between the creamy mint center and the soft, chocolatey shell produces a sensory experience that plays with flavor and texture. These packed cookies prove the limitless opportunities for creativity in the baking industry, especially with their unexpected minty pop.

As we end our investigation into creative and modern cookie recipes with a minty touch, it is clear that baking is an open platform for innovation and research. Every cookie variety, from the traditional chocolate chip to the upscale ginger-mint snap, offers a distinctive interplay of flavors and textures beyond the typical. By adding a layer of freshness and excitement to the familiar, whether through extracts, fresh herbs, or unusual pairings, the infusion of mint elevates the ordinary cookie to the status of culinary art.

There are countless opportunities for reinvention in the kitchen, where tradition and innovation collide. These fresh and imaginative cookie recipes highlight the many mint uses while encouraging prospective bakers to explore their artistic side. To celebrate the enjoyment of reimagining classics and relishing the surprises that arise from the union of tradition and invention, preheat the oven, assemble your ingredients, and let the aromatic magic of mint-infused cookies fill your kitchen.

Unique flavor combinations and surprising ingredients

The culinary arts are a large and dynamic field where innovation is unrestricted. Unusual and flavor combinations are the critical components of culinary innovation; these alchemical components turn everyday meals into spectacular culinary experiences. This section takes the reader on a sensory adventure as we explore the skill of combining unusual flavors and ingredients in novel ways that both test the palette and expand the definition of gourmet delight.

Culinary creativity is typified by the deft juxtaposition of disparate tastes, which results in fascinating and unexpected flavor combinations. Consider the combination of sweet and savory flavors in a dish that combines the sharpness of Granny Smith apples with the luscious, honey-glazed pork. Each flavor enhances the others in a ballet of tastes that goes beyond the individual ingredients, thanks to the synergy of flavors.

This sweet-savory combination displays the transforming power of blending seemingly dissimilar flavors while tantalizing the taste buds.

Beyond the norm, combining umami-rich products with sweet counterparts creates culinary exploration opportunities. Imagine a dish that combines lush, juicy strawberries with plump, juicy tomatoes—a startling combination that combines the inherent sweetness of strawberries with the savory depth of tomatoes. This surprising blend of flavors disproves stereotypes and demonstrates how ingredients can create a symphony of flavors that enhances the dining experience.

The realm of herbs and spices offers a creative space for individuals exploring distinct taste profiles. Imagine a dish where the zesty, bright tones of coriander blend perfectly with cumin's warm, earthy flavors. This combination of spices complicates the dish and shows how various culinary herbs and spices may create unexpected flavor combinations. These pairings arouse the senses and entice guests to relish the complex layers of flavors interwoven in every mouthful.

Combining typically sweet drinks with savory and herbal aromas adds complexity and mystery to the beverage world. Imagine a drink that mixes the herbaceous freshness of simple syrup infused with rosemary and mezcal's smoky depth. The surprising fusion of the strong and the delicate results in a beyond-ordinary drink and takes the palate on a sensory adventure through unexplored flavor lands.

The skill of culinary inventiveness is further enhanced by unexpected components that are thoughtfully chosen and incorporated. When it comes to desserts, adding olive oil to a traditional chocolate cake gives it a savory, complex depth. This dish is rich and elegant without being overly so. The richness of the olive oil tempers the sweetness of the chocolate. This switch from conventional baking fats demonstrates the ability of unexpected components to redefine tried-and-true recipes completely.

Unexpected additions are often welcome in the savory domain; a good example is adding coffee grinds to a spice rub for grilled meats. A depth of flavor that stays on the mouth is created by the rich, bitter overtones enhancing the smokiness of the grill and the gritty texture of the coffee grounds, which add a wonderful crunch. This creative application of coffee grinds as a savory component highlights how cutting-edge contemporary cooking methods are.

Stepping outside the world of fruits and veggies, the flavor combination of watermelon and feta cheese is unexpectedly harmonic. The saline salinity of feta contrasts with watermelon's juicy, refreshing sweetness to create a visually stunning and satisfying salad. This surprising combination pushes the bounds of conventional flavor profiles and gives the idea of fruit-based salads a delicious spin.

As chefs strive to push the frontiers of flavor exploration, the culinary world has also seen an increase in the use of foraged and unusual ingredients. Consider the application of edible flowers in salads and sweets, like pansies or nasturtiums. These blossoms' delicate, flowery overtones enhance the overall dining experience by adding subtle flavors in addition to aesthetic appeal. This acceptance of unusual and foraged ingredients is a nod back to the early days of culinary exploration when cooks drew inspiration from the abundance of nature.

Combining components from many culinary traditions creates many exciting opportunities in global cuisines. Imagine a dish that marries the smokey heat of chipotle chiles with the umami-rich flavors of miso, a union of Mexican and Japanese influences that results in a savory, spicy, and sweet note symphony. This cross- cultural investigation is a prime example of how gastronomy constantly changes, with cooks creating meals that cut across cultural barriers by drawing influence from various culinary traditions.

It becomes clear that culinary invention involves intuition, exploration, and technique as we negotiate the landscape of unusual flavor combinations and ingredients. Both home cooks and chefs draw inspiration from the unexpected, daring to try out sensations that push the boundaries of taste and reinvent culinary conventions. The emerging field of molecular gastronomy, in which chefs utilize scientific concepts to dissect and reinvent well-known foods in novel and eye-catching ways, is a prime example of this attitude of research.

In summary, the culinary arts are a creative canvas, and the uncommon ingredients and inventive flavor combinations act as the paintbrushes that bring culinary masterpieces to life. The culinary landscape is constantly changing, driven by the curious minds and fearless palates of people who strive to push the frontiers of taste. Examples include the surprising pairing of sweet and savory and the use of unusual ingredients like coffee grounds and edible flowers. Let us embrace the thrill of gastronomic exploration and relish the delicious discoveries that arise when tradition meets innovation in the field of the unexpected as we celebrate the alchemy of flavor.

Showcasing how traditional recipes can be reinvented for a contemporary audience

The nexus of tradition and innovation in the dynamic field of gastronomy serves as a rich source of culinary creativity. Generation after generation of cooks have handed down traditional recipes rich in cultural legacy and culinary history. But the true nature of culinary art is to reimagine these traditions for a modern audience and keep them alive. This section explores the fascinating topic of modernizing classic recipes, showing how home cooks and chefs alike can update beloved meals to appeal to the tastes and sensitivities of today's discriminating diners.

Though the comforting and nostalgic qualities of traditional recipes make them beloved, the dynamic nature of culinary arts permits adaptation without sacrificing authenticity. Consider the classic Italian dish, spaghetti Bolognese. Although based on the rustic Italian flavors, modern chefs add a contemporary twist using plant-based substitutes. In addition to satisfying the increasing need for plant-based alternatives, replacing meat with robust lentils or mushrooms adds a rich flavor that appeals to the changing tastes of an environmentally and health-sensitive modern audience.

Regarding comfort food, the simple macaroni and cheese takes on new life as cooks play around with different cheese combinations and handmade pasta. The traditional mac and cheese is elevated to a gourmet experience by combining aged Gouda, sharp cheddar, and a hint of truffle oil. This reimagining retains the soul of a cherished recipe and welcomes a new wave of foodies to enjoy the tried-and-true from a different angle.

Reimagining classic dishes goes beyond changing ingredients to include the cooking method. One of the best examples is the traditional method of slow cooking. While classic stews and braises took hours to simmer on the stove, modern versions use the effectiveness of quick pots and slow cookers. This contemporary method accommodates the time constraints of a fast-paced lifestyle while maintaining the richness of flavors and tenderness associated with slow-cooked food.

A broad mix of culinary heritages is often required to adapt classic recipes, and global culinary traditions offer a rich tapestry of flavors. The traditional Japanese sushi roll is creatively transformed when it comes into contact with the bright flavors of Latin America. The sushi burrito is a clever combination of rice, avocado, and fresh fish that is covered in seaweed. In addition to showcasing the interaction between Japanese and Latin American cuisines, this culinary hybrid meets the modern need for portable and easily transportable solutions.

Traditionally made desserts also see a resurgence as pastry chefs give traditional delicacies a modern twist. Usually filled with vanilla or chocolate pastry cream, the French éclair is given a new lease on life by innovative fillings such as matcha-infused custard or passion fruit curd. The reimagining of éclairs appeals to a global palate that is greedy for novel and varied flavor experiences while also honoring the artistry of French pastry.

Reimagining classic dishes frequently requires balancing maintaining authenticity and utilizing cutting-edge cooking methods. When it comes to the traditional Spanish meal paella, modern cooks experiment with different grains like quinoa or farro, adding a nutrient-rich touch while honoring the dish's heritage. Proteins prepared using sous-vide methods are guaranteed to be perfectly done while keeping tradition and utilizing the accuracy of contemporary technology.

Professional chefs can reimagine classic recipes; home cooks are also integral to this culinary revolution. Family recipes are passed down with a distinct touch in kitchens worldwide, whether it's the inclusion of a unique spice blend or the replacement of a customary item with one that can be found locally. Through this grassroots reinvention, culinary traditions are preserved and given the flexibility to adjust to the constantly shifting tastes of society.

The influence of seasonal and regional ingredients further enhances the reinterpretation of ancient recipes. The traditional Greek salad in Mediterranean cooking changes with the seasons, substituting robust root vegetables for juicy summer tomatoes and cucumbers. This adaptation shows that chefs are aware of the environmental impact of their resources and demonstrates their inventiveness in creating dishes that capture the season's essence.

Understanding the importance of cultural sensitivity and respect is crucial as we investigate the reinventing of ancient recipes. When done with consideration, blending culinary traditions promotes intercultural understanding and highlights the diversity of world cuisine. For instance, tofu or tempeh is used in a vegetarian version of the classic beef-based Korean meal bibimbap. This accommodates dietary requirements and combines modern plant-based options with traditional Korean flavors.

The culinary arts are dynamic, as evidenced by the reimagining of classic recipes. It's a kind of art that feeds on innovation, a readiness to push limits, and a grasp of the changing preferences of a modern audience. Reinvention gives culinary traditions new life, whether in the hands of talented chefs in Michelin- starred restaurants or the home cook tinkering with a treasured family recipe.

In summary, reimagining classic dishes is an homage to the dynamic interplay between innovation and tradition in culinary history. It's an acknowledgment that the spirit of a dish may be maintained while embracing the transforming force of global influences, contemporary methods, and a heightened consciousness of sustainability and health. Let us honor the chefs, home cooks, and food lovers who, with every inventive twist and surprising turn, add to the vivid tapestry of flavors that define the constantly evolving world of gastronomy as we enjoy the fruits of this culinary Renaissance.

CHAPTER V

Gluten-Free and Vegan Options

Catering to dietary preferences with delicious gluten-free and vegan minty cookies

The difficulty of making delights that satisfy everyone has grown more apparent in the modern culinary scene when dietary preferences range over a spectrum as broad as the human palate itself. Dietary choices such as gluten-free and vegan are growing in popularity, motivated by the desire to make ethical and health- conscious decisions. This section delves into the world of sugary delight, examining the artistry of creating mouthwatering vegan and gluten-free minty cookies that
satisfy dietary requirements while providing a fantastic flavor profile.

Because the traditional idea of cookies is based on wheat, butter, and eggs, it presents a unique set of difficulties in meeting the dietary requirements of those who are vegan or gluten-free. But for inventive bakers, the growing array of substitute ingredients presents many opportunities. Almond flour is a highly adaptable and nutrient-dense alternative when baking without gluten. Its finely ground texture offers a delicate crumb reminiscent of classic cookies, and the nutty flavor harmonizes with the minty infusion to create a pleasing combination suitable for those with gluten sensitivities.

Regarding vegan diets, the lack of animal products means that creative substitutions for butter and eggs are required. Here's where coconut oil and flaxseed or chia seed "eggs" come in. These two ingredients combine to provide the moisture and binding qualities that make a cookie successful. This vegan version maintains the classic soft and chewy feel that characterizes a delicious cookie while adhering to ethical eating practices.

These gluten-free and vegan recipes gain complexity from mint's refreshing and invigorating flavor. The flavorful leaves of the peppermint plant are used to make peppermint extract, which gives the cookies a refreshing, chilly taste that entices the palate. Almond flour, coconut oil, and peppermint essence combine to create a cookie that is not only delicious but also satisfies dietary requirements by providing a beautiful harmony of flavors and textures.

Adding dark chocolate chunks or chips adds a delicious touch and enhances the overall richness of the biscuit. The sweet and minty scent blends well with the bitter notes of dark chocolate to create a sophisticated yet decadent balance. Carefully chosen premium dark chocolate guarantees a vegan- and gluten-free addition that enhances the overall texture of the cookie.

The perfume of freshly made mint-infused cookies fills the kitchen, and these delicious, vegan, and gluten-free cookies appeal to people who don't follow rigid diets. All cookie lovers are drawn to them, urging them to experience the creativity and attention to detail that goes into creating delights that satisfy various dietary requirements. The skill of creating vegan and gluten-free minty cookies is a celebration of inclusivity, allowing everyone to enjoy the delight of a freshly baked cookie without having to make any dietary compromises.

Commercial baking has shifted due to the growing demand for vegan and gluten-free choices outside residential kitchens. Recognizing how important it is to accommodate a range of dietary requirements, bakeries and confectioneries have created inclusive delights without sacrificing quality or taste. Formerly a specialty item, gluten-free and vegan minty cookies are now commonplace in the showcases of progressive businesses, demonstrating a dedication to delivering alternatives to all patrons, irrespective of their dietary preferences.

The allure of these vegan and gluten-free minty cookies extends beyond dietary limitations and encompasses a more comprehensive perspective on leading a health-conscious lifestyle. These sweets' thoughtful ingredient selection attracts many people, whether motivated by a desire for cleaner eating, gluten sensitivity, or ethical concerns. The lack of animal products, refined flours, and artificial additives aligns with holistic health, providing a guilt-free treatment that satisfies both the body and the conscience.

In the social fabric of contemporary society, where events frequently bring together people with various dietary requirements, having gluten-free and vegan goodies on hand promotes inclusivity. With no worries about nutritional limitations, friends and family may enjoy a shared dessert together thanks to these minty cookies, which serve as a unifying factor. Baking and distributing vegan and gluten-free snacks is a considerate act that recognizes and honors the variety of dietary preferences in the community.

Success with these vegan and gluten-free minty cookies depends on selecting substitute components and techniques. It takes a sophisticated knowledge of plant-based fats, natural sweeteners, and gluten-free flours to get the ideal moisture, texture, and flavor ratio. As bakers experiment with ratios, temperatures, and baking times to guarantee that every batch of cookies comes out of the oven with the appropriate characteristics—soft, chewy, and bursting with delicious mint flavor—baking science transforms into an art form.

The inventive possibilities of baking using gluten-free and vegan ingredients are not limited to cookies; they can be applied to various baked products, such as cakes and pastries. Creative bakers are exploring and expanding the possibilities of gluten-free and vegan pastry arts in response to the growing demand for inclusive solutions. The key to these efforts' success is their commitment to taste, texture, and presentation, which guarantees that vegan and gluten-free sweets are magnificent works of art unto themselves rather than just acceptable alternatives.

To sum up, creating mouthwatering minty cookies free of gluten and veganism goes beyond following dietary guidelines and becomes a celebration of creative cooking. Combining unconventional ingredients, careful baking techniques, and a dedication to inclusion yields delicacies pleasing to a wide range of palates. These cookies prove how cuisine is changing, with inventiveness and deference to different dietary requirements coming together to redefine what can be indulged in. We celebrate not just a moment of gastronomic pleasure but also a sign of inclusivity and appreciation for the variety of options that determine our modern attitude to eating as we relish the minty freshness of these gluten-free and vegan delicacies.

Tips on ingredient substitutions and maintaining flavor integrity

A competent chef or home cook must be able to adapt and improvise in the ever-changing world of culinary arts. In this culinary alchemy, ingredient substitutions are essential because they provide cooks flexibility to create dishes that accommodate dietary needs, allergies, or just the availability of particular items. However, there are difficulties in the art of substitution, especially when preserving flavor integrity. This section delves into the complex realm of ingredient substitutions, examining methods and approaches to guarantee that the flavor profile of a dish is maintained despite ingredient changes.

When replacing ingredients, one of the most important things to remember is how each item affects the dish's overall flavor character. Consider the delicate warmth and complexity that cinnamon adds to a dish. If you can't get cinnamon, nutmeg or allspice would work well in its place, each with its subtle flavor characteristics. To ensure that the desired flavor profile is preserved, the secret is to determine the principal attribute of the component that needs to be replaced and choose a substitute that matches or enhances that quality.

The choice of leavening agents can significantly impact the final product's texture and taste, especially in baking, where accuracy is crucial. It is essential to consider whether the recipe calls for acidic or alkaline ingredients when replacing baking soda with baking powder. Suppose the recipe calls for an acidic ingredient like buttermilk or yogurt. In that case, baking soda can be used instead of baking powder, a mixture of an acid (typically cream of tartar) and a base (usually baking soda). Cooks knowledgeable about the chemistry of leavening agents are better equipped to substitute ingredients without upsetting the delicate flavor balance.

Dairy products are frequently essential in providing various foods, from savory sauces to sumptuous sweets, and their richness and creaminess. But for people who are lactose intolerant or who are vegan, you have to find appropriate replacements. Dairy milk can be substituted with coconut, almond, or soy milk, which have comparable creamy textures and distinct flavor characteristics. Olive oil or vegan butter can be used instead of regular butter in savory recipes to maintain the desired richness without sacrificing flavor.

The selection of fats during cooking can elevate a dish from average to exceptional. It's essential to consider how fat substitutions, such as olive oil for butter, can affect texture and flavor. Butter adds a creamy richness, while olive oil adds a fruity, slightly peppery aroma that enhances dish depth. Cooks are more equipped to make replacements that improve a dish's overall flavor profile and texture when they are aware of the unique qualities of fats.

Regarding sweeteners, the trend toward healthier options has led many people to look into refined sugar alternatives. In many recipes, you can use honey, maple syrup, agave nectar, or even fruit purees in place of sugar. Each substitution adds a distinct sweetness and more taste layers, enhancing the dish's richness and depth. However, it's essential to pay attention to the moisture content of liquid sweeteners and modify the recipe's total liquid ratio appropriately.

Due to their flavor-enhancing and aromatic qualities, herbs and spices are frequently the essence of a cuisine. However, inventive substitutes can maintain the flavor profile even when a particular herb or spice is unavailable. To keep the earthy and herbaceous elements in a savory recipe, thyme could be used instead of rosemary. Cumin adds a toasty, somewhat lemony note like coriander, which can be substituted in some recipes. To prevent overpowering the dish, it's essential to select alternatives with flavor profiles comparable to your original while also considering the substitute's intensity.

Due to their zesty, citrus fruits are often used in savory and sweet recipes. In situations where a particular citrus fruit is unavailable, inventive alternatives can be utilized. For example, lime can be used in many recipes instead of lemon or vice versa without affecting overall flavor integrity. Orange zest can also be used instead of lemon zest to give the meal a zesty freshness. While maintaining the ideal flavor balance, culinary diversity can be achieved by adjusting to the available citrus alternatives.

There are many options in the realm of grains for substitutes that meet dietary requirements or tastes. Quinoa flour or rice flour can be used instead of regular wheat flour in various recipes for individuals looking for gluten-free options. These substitutes' earthy and nutty overtones enrich the dish's overall flavor profile, making the substitution a culinary improvement rather than merely a dietary need. Cooks can better choose replacements that complement the desired flavor profile when they know the subtle differences in flavor between various grains.

Working with proteins presents a unique set of difficulties when substituting animal-based products, particularly in the context of vegetarian or vegan diets. But there are now new options thanks to the development of plant-based proteins and animal substitutes. In savory recipes, tofu, tempeh, or seitan can be used in place of typical meats to provide a variety of textures and absorb the meal's flavors. Egg white substitutes in desserts, such as aquafaba (chickpea brine), work well as a binding agent without sacrificing flavor.

Generally speaking, while changing an ingredient,

It's best to taste as you go and start with modest amounts. This enables modifications to be made as needed, guaranteeing that the finished dish will match individual tastes and the desired flavor profile. Keeping an open mind and being eager to try new things also promotes culinary research, which can result in discovering exciting and delicious pairings that could become signature dishes in one's repertoire.

To sum up, one of the most dynamic and inventive aspects of culinary proficiency is the skill of component substitution. A competent chef can easily traverse the realm of substitutes, staying true to the essence of a dish's flavor character while accommodating dietary restrictions or reacting to ingredient shortages. By knowing each ingredient's properties and selecting appropriate substitutes, chefs can boldly go on a culinary adventure that embraces flexibility without sacrificing flavor integrity. When handled creatively and with understanding, the alchemy of component replacements creates a monument to the limitless possibilities in the kitchen, where flavor discovery is unrestricted.

Ensuring everyone can enjoy a cool and minty Christmas delight

The moments spent with loved ones around the Christmas table turn into the focal point of the season as the festivities deepen and the air is filled with the promise of joy and celebration. Flavors are a significant part of the rich tapestry of holiday customs, and mint's refreshing, excellent essence stands out as a classic Christmas treat. But as we get together with loved ones, ensuring everyone at the table can enjoy the holiday delights becomes more crucial than ever. To make the holiday celebrations genuinely exceptional for everyone, we examine in this section the art of creating cool and minty Christmas delicacies that are delicious and inclusive, accommodating various dietary choices and constraints.

With its white and dark chocolate layers, the traditional peppermint bark has come to be associated with the holidays. However, the presence of dairy and conventional chocolate presents a problem for people on vegan or lactose-free diets. Welcome to the era of chocolate made from plants and dairy substitutes. Bakers can produce a rich and decadent peppermint bark that keeps all the seasonal charm without sacrificing flavor by using premium vegan chocolate and coconut oil. Crushed candy canes add the perfect minty crunch, finishing off a treat that embodies the inclusive spirit of the holiday season.

The traditional candy cane-shaped cookies are uniquely positioned in the holiday baking repertoire within the baked goods category. However, people following vegan or gluten-free diets may find the classic buttery cookie base an obstacle. Bakers can guarantee that everyone can savor the whimsical enjoyment of candy cane cookies by using gluten-free flour mixes and accepting alternative fats like coconut oil. A coating of powdered sugar on top and the infusion of peppermint flavor produce a sensory experience that embodies the spirit of Christmas and invites everyone to enjoy the wonder of the season.

The thought of a creamy and minty hot chocolate adds another level of satisfaction for those who enjoy hot chocolate's warm, comforting embrace on a cold Christmas evening. However, people who are lactose intolerant or follow a vegan diet may find it challenging to utilize chocolate and milk derived from dairy. Smoothly substituting traditional dairy with almond, coconut, or oat milk will result in a velvety texture that accentuates the richness of dark chocolate. An excellent, refreshing twist is added by infusing peppermint extract or a minty syrup, turning the traditional hot chocolate into a Christmas treat that many enjoy. With its recognizable mint flavor and red and white stripes, the candy cane has become an iconic image of Christmas. But candy canes with natural flavors and without added coloring can be made vegan using raw food dyes and substitute sweeteners. Candy makers can create candies that align with a broader range of dietary choices by utilizing organic cane sugar or maple syrup instead of beet juice or other plant-based colorings. Not only do these handmade treats decorate stockings and Christmas trees, but they also stand for dedication to thoughtful craftsmanship and inclusivity.

Amidst the array of holiday pies and tarts, the dessert with peppermint flavor is an excellent alternative. However, many dishes' buttery crust and cream-filled layers could be difficult for someone following a strict diet. Bakers may make a minty masterpiece that accommodates a range of dietary demands by experimenting with gluten-free pie crusts produced from alternative flours like almond or coconut flour and swapping out dairy-based creams with cashew or coconut equivalents. A dash of peppermint-infused syrup or fresh mint leaves gives a blast of flavor that elevates the dessert to a classy and elegant Christmas treat.

While there will be a variety of goodies on the holiday table, people who follow low-sugar or diabetic-friendly diets also need to consider dietary limitations. Because traditional holiday desserts are sometimes loaded with sugar, it can be difficult for people following nutritional restrictions to enjoy the sweet festivities. Nonetheless, chilly, minty treats without much sugar can be made with natural sweeteners like stevia or monk fruit. The world of festive snacks is expanding to include individuals looking for a healthier but still delicious indulgence. Examples of these treats include sugar-free peppermint patties and mint-flavored chocolate truffles sweetened with alternatives.

Beyond dietary restrictions, the inclusiveness extends to those with nut allergies, a common issue around the holidays. While nuts contribute taste and texture to many traditional Christmas dishes, substitutes like seeds, coconut flakes, or gluten-free oats can also add a pleasant crunch. In addition to guaranteeing the safety of individuals with nut allergies, the thoughtful ingredient selection adds novel and intriguing textures that enrich the celebration treats' entire sensory experience.

Christmas goodies should be included for people controlling their gluten intake. Although wheat-based flours are used in many traditional desserts, gluten-free flour alternatives make it possible to create delicacies suitable for all dietary preferences. Bakers can experiment with various flours to create delights that will make everyone on the festive table happy, from gluten-free peppermint brownies to cakes made with almond flour infused with mint.

The frozen dessert industry is viable in pursuing all-encompassing, chilly, and minty Christmas sweets. Developing peppermint ice creams or sorbets free of gluten and dairy offers a revitalizing and festive option for those seeking a cold indulgence. The creamy basis of these frozen treats may be made vegan using coconut milk, almond milk, or other non-dairy milk substitutes. The addition of chocolate chunks or chips and the hint of peppermint make them sophisticated enough to serve at any holiday gathering.

To sum up, the delicious treats that adorn the holiday table are just as much a part of the magic of Christmas as the sparkling lights, cozy laughing, and thoughtful gift-giving. Making refreshing, minty Christmas confections that suit a range of dietary requirements reflects the inclusive, welcoming nature of the holiday. When chefs and bakers set out to create holiday treats, they should carefully examine the ingredients to make Christmas accessible to everyone. This will help create lasting memories after consuming the last bite of delicious peppermint candy.

CHAPTER VI

Decorative Techniques

Step-by-step guide to decorating cool and minty cookies

Cookie decorating is a skill that goes beyond the basic process of baking, turning tasty cookies into visually stunning and aesthetically pleasing edible works of art. The appeal of chilled, minty cookies takes center stage as the Christmas season approaches, adding a welcome touch to the repertory of festive desserts. This section takes us on a tour of the world of cookie decoration, revealing a systematic approach that teaches the abilities required to garnish cookies with a minty touch and takes the fun of preparing cookies for the holidays to a whole new level.

Making the ideal canvas—a cookie with the correct texture, flavor, and structural integrity—is the cornerstone of any exquisitely adorned cookie. Start by deciding on a dependable cookie recipe that complements the flavor character you want. Try a mint-infused sugar cookie or a traditional sugar cookie for refreshing, minty treats. Roll out the cookie dough to a consistent thickness to ensure even baking. Cut the dough into festive shapes using cookie cutters that represent the season's spirit—be it candy canes, snowflakes, or merry Santas. Allow the cookies to cool completely before beginning the decorating frenzy after baking them until the edges turn brown.

The icing, a versatile material that adds a coating of sweetness and flavor and acts as an adhesive for edible embellishments, is the next essential component in the cookie decorating process. Melt the meringue powder, add the water to the powdered sugar, and mix until you get a smooth and colorful minty royal frosting. Mix the ingredients with a whisk until the icing becomes thick but pourable. If you use multiple icing colors, divide it into separate bowls. To ensure that every bite of the icing has the essence of the season, add peppermint
extract to give it a cold, pleasant, minty flavor.

The secret to making gorgeously decorated cookies is to become proficient in the outline and flooding processes. Outline the edges of each biscuit with the minty royal icing using a piping bag fitted with a tiny round tip. This gives your patterns a defined shape and forms a barrier to confine the flooding icing. After the outlines are set, dilute the leftover icing with water to make it more pourable. Spread the thinned icing evenly over the indicated area using a tiny spoon or a squeeze bottle. Use a toothpick or scribe tool to ensure a flat surface and guide the icing into corners. Let the flooded icing set before adding the next layer or design feature.
Try stacking different colors and textures to give your minty cookies more depth and visual appeal. If you want to create a gradient look, try blending complementary hues like white and chocolate brown or using different tones of mint green. To add texture, use various pipe tips to create swirls, lines, or dots. Because royal icing is so versatile, it may make intricate details like the colorful swirls of peppermint candies or the delicate lines of snowflakes. Let each layer set entirely before adding the next to keep the colors sharp and vivid.

No frosted cookie would be complete without a few edible decorations to give it flair and depth. For a pop of color and texture, try adding finely crushed candy canes or peppermint candies to your minty cookies. While the icing is still wet, sprinkle these decorations over the cookies so they stick. Alternatively, you can evoke the icy appeal of winter by adding edible glitter or shimmering dust. Create a tactile and visual feast for the senses by experimenting with various textures, such as the softness of edible pearls and the crunch of
sanding sugar.

You can add unique touches to your minty cookies that highlight your ingenuity by piping embellishments and accents for more detailed decorations, such as snowflakes, festive greetings, or holly leaves, and conduct significant amounts of royal icing. Invest in various piping tips to create multiple designs, such as elaborate lace patterns or thin lines. Piping allows you to enhance the visual appeal of your cookies by adding three-dimensional components like raised bows or rosettes. Let the piped details be set fully before handling or packing to avoid smearing.

After adding layers of frosting, colors, and edible decorations to your minty cookies, the last step is to ensure they are presented carefully and wrapped to preserve freshness. Let the decorated cookies dry completely—ideally overnight- to avoid smudging— before stacking or packing. After the cookies have dried, carefully move them to airtight jars or place them in festive boxes, ensuring that every artwork is safe and prepared for sharing or giving. Think about tying ribbons or affixing handmade tags with good wishes for the season to add festive charm.

To summarize, creating cold and minty cookies is a fun process that blends culinary skill and artistic expression. Every stage of the process, from the first creation of the ideal cookie canvas to the painstaking layering of colors and detailing, adds to the enchantment of delicious holiday art. The excitement for bakers as they embark on this creative journey comes from the final products' exquisite appearance and the memories and moments spent together around the holiday table. Crafted with love and imagination, these minty delights become more
than just festive treats—they're delicious
representations of the warmth and magic that
characterize the holiday season.

Using peppermint-themed designs and colors to enhance the festive spirit

As the holiday season progresses, decoration takes center stage in both homes and public areas, and the air fills with the aroma of evergreens and the promise of celebrations. Peppermint is a classic and revitalizing theme that pleases the palate and the eyes among the many seasonal motifs. This section delves into the fascinating realm of peppermint-themed patterns and hues, revealing how these components elevate the festive mood and add a refined touch to the holiday festivities.

Peppermint candies' distinctive red and white stripes make them readily identifiable and arouse sentimental feelings connected to seasonal customs. Using these traditional hues in holiday décor gives rooms a timeless appeal that reminds people of their best childhood Christmas memories. Red and white linens on table settings and peppermint-inspired ornaments on tree decorations are just two examples of how these colors work together to create a cohesive, eye-catching atmosphere that perfectly captures the season's essence.

Patterns with a peppermint theme can be seen in many other seasonal aspects, not just candies. Peppermint themes in holiday décor, from elaborately crafted tree decorations to joyous wreaths and garlands, create a sense of coherence and thematic harmony. A peppermint candy's characteristic spiral is used as a recurring pattern to embellish everything from gift wrap to ribbons, weaving a coherent visual narrative that connects the many components of holiday décor.

Because peppermint themes are so adaptable, holiday décor may be personalized and creatively designed. Red and white stripes are an essential and timeless design element that may be combined with various complementary colors to fit personal preferences. A touch of luxury is added by combining peppermint designs with silver or gold accents, and the classic Christmas hues are harmoniously blended with green foliage and natural features. Because of its versatility, peppermint-themed décor can easily fit in with current holiday customs while allowing for plenty of individual expression.

The dining table becomes a canvas for creative expression inspired by peppermint, with dishware, napkins, and tablecloths exhibiting the eye-catching red and white color scheme. Using placemats or table runners with peppermint stripes adds a festive touch and makes a striking backdrop for holiday meals and get-togethers. Whether they are candy-filled jars or peppermint-scented candles, peppermint-themed centerpieces act as focal points that encapsulate the spirit of the season, beckoning friends and family to assemble around a table decked out in coziness and warmth.

Peppermint's enchantment also reaches the kitchen, where holiday sweets become more than just delicious treats—they become pieces of beauty. Desserts with a peppermint flavor and red and white accents highlight the season's elegant theme. Adding peppermint flavors and designs turns sweets like candy cane-shaped cookies and layered peppermint bark into palatable representations of seasonal cheer. Every bite is a visual and gustatory extravaganza, thanks to the utilization of red and white icing and crushed peppermint candy decorations.

Peppermint greeting cards and holiday stationery themes add a sophisticated yet whimsical touch. These designs bring a thoughtful touch to holiday correspondence, whether the subtle peppermint highlights on festive letterhead or the red and white stripes framing a family photo on a personalized card. Gift tags and wrapping section with peppermint designs further improve gift presentation, resulting in a unified and eye-catching package that conveys the thought and care put into giving.

When peppermint-themed outdoor decor is used, homes' exteriors are transformed into a winter paradise. These decorations, ranging from enormous candy cane decorations to pathway lights with peppermint stripes, add to the festive mood and encourage neighbors and onlookers to join in the spirit of the holidays. Wreaths and garlands are adorned with peppermint-colored ribbons and bows, which provide a splash of color against the backdrop of wintry scenes. These designs' whimsical elegance perfectly captures the whimsical spirit of the season and results in a warm and inviting exterior.

During the holidays, peppermint-inspired motifs often appear in accessories and clothing. From warm scarves with stripes of red and white to socks with a peppermint design, these accessories become tangible manifestations of joyous celebration. Holiday sweaters and clothes with peppermint themes give a whimsical element to seasonal outfits, enabling people to celebrate the season's spirit in style. The traditional pairing of red and white turns into a seasonal fashion statement, establishing a visual link between people and the joyous atmosphere around them.

The peppermint theme carries over to holiday get-togethers and parties when guests' experience is improved by well-thought-out décor. Tablecloths, napkins, and drinkware with peppermint stripes make a unified and eye-catching arrangement. Invitations with a peppermint pattern created the mood for the occasion and gave guests a preview of the joyous celebration. Every little element helps create enduring memories, and peppermint-inspired centerpieces and party favors add even more charm.

In summary, peppermint-themed patterns and hues throughout the Christmas season go beyond simple aesthetics to serve as a visual language that conveys the happiness, coziness, and time-honored customs connected to the holiday. These patterns lend a timeless beauty to holiday décor that appeals to people of all ages, whether complex peppermint candy patterns or simple red and white stripes. By adding peppermint-inspired decorations to our homes, tables, and clothing, we celebrate the holiday spirit and establish a common visual language that unites us in the season's beauty.

With its unique hues and patterns, peppermint transcends beyond its use as a theme to represent the everlasting wonder and joy that characterize the holiday season.

Tips for creating visually stunning treats without compromising on taste

The proverb "We eat with our eyes first" applies to gastronomic delights, highlighting the significance of aesthetic appeal in enhancing the overall dining experience. But the quest of designing aesthetically pleasing confections shouldn't sacrifice flavor; instead, it's an art form that skillfully combines flavor and aesthetics. To ensure the pleasure of enjoying a dish is as much a visual flavor as a gustatory delight, we will explore various strategies and techniques for creating delicacies that captivate the eyes and delight the palate in this section.

Carefully choosing premium ingredients is the cornerstone of any visually spectacular dessert. The finest chocolates, aromatic spices, and seasonal vegetables are the cornerstones that provide the foundation for both gastronomic and visual perfection. Edible flowers, herbs, and vibrant fruits all contribute subtle qualities that balance the overall flavor profile and add a pop of color. Selecting ingredients at the height of their freshness guarantees that the dessert has a rich flavor that lingers in the mouth and a pleasing appearance.

Creating aesthetically spectacular food heavily relies on presentation art. A basic dish can become a delicious work of art with careful plating or platter presentation. When plating, consider the visual harmony of hues, textures, and shapes, striving for a visually appealing arrangement. Every component, whether a sauce drizzle, a powdered sugar dusting, or the thoughtful arrangement of garnishes, adds to the dish's overall aesthetic coherence. Accept the plate's canvas as a vital component of the eating experience, which lets the delicacy be presented in all its visual glory.

Treats' visual appeal is greatly influenced by color, and the creative application of a varied palette can improve the entire design. Play with various colors, using naturally colorful foods like leafy greens, citrus fruits, and berries. When choosing ingredients for a recipe, consider the color wheel and look for complementary or contrasting hues to provide visual flair. Edible flowers elevate an otherwise ordinary treat to a piece of art by adding a splash of color and a delicate and elegant touch.

Another element that adds to the visual appeal of snacks is texture. Interacting crispy, creamy textures and smooth, crunchy parts produces a dynamic tactile and visual experience. Try layering different components, such as crispy almonds, creamy sauces, or delicate meringues, to give the dessert more depth and complexity. The juxtaposition of textures elevates the visual appeal and overall sensory experience, transforming each bite into a voyage of flavors and feelings.

Treats are elevated by the skill of dripping and swirling, which also makes them aesthetically stunning. Whether it's a fruity coulis, a delicate glaze, or a rich chocolate ganache, the thoughtful use of these ingredients improves the dish's appearance and flavor. Use a Flavor fork or piping bag to make elaborate patterns, swirls, or zigzags that enhance the composition. In addition to creating visual interest, the skillful pouring of sauces offers a taste dimension that complements the dish.

Using edible embellishments and decorations allows for customization and inventiveness. Anything from chocolate curls to edible gold leaf can be used as ornamental elements to turn a dessert into an eye-catching work of art. When selecting decorations, please consider the dish's concept and flavor profile to make sure they complement the composition rather than detract from it. In addition to being aesthetically pleasing, edible flowers, microgreens, and herb sprigs add subdued flavors that go well with the main elements.

Experiment with forms and shapes to make visually appealing and delectable desserts. Try using cookie cutters, molds, or even free-form sculpting to give your projects a distinctive look that will stick in their memory. A touch of surprise and refinement is added by carefully arranging bite-sized candies or building complex layers. By defying convention and utilizing non-traditional shapes, sweets become eatable sculptures that arouse curiosity even before a bite.

Because it provides another level of visual appeal, think about the vessel or container in which the treat is delivered. The serving vessel selection affects the overall look, from sophisticated dessert plates to rustic wooden boards. Use unusual containers like glass jars, slate boards, or hollowed-out fruits to make an eye-catching display. The container not only sets the scene for the dessert but also improves the overall theme and atmosphere of the meal.

It's essential to recognize that lighting plays a significant part in producing visually appealing food. A dish's colors and textures can be emphasized with thoughtful lighting, making an eye-catching visual presentation. When natural light isn't available, try using gentle ambient lighting to create a cozy and welcoming ambiance. Natural light is best for displaying the actual colors of the treat. Consider highlighting particular treat components with spotlights or directional lighting to emphasize their eye-catching characteristics.

Treats get additional charm when storytelling and theme components are included, turning them into narrative experiences. Treats with a thematic concept infuse the senses more deeply, whether a complex creation inspired by a cultural heritage or a fanciful dessert inspired by a storybook. To create an immersive dining experience that immerses diners in a world where visual and gustatory pleasures are combined, think of using objects, themed backgrounds, or even music to go along with the experience.

Thoughtfully chosen portion amounts enhance the aesthetic balance of a dish. Although decadent confections are frequently connected to excess, moderation guarantees that excess does not detract from aesthetic appeal. Try small servings, micro versions, or creative plating that present the pleasure in a visually appealing but not overpowering way. A sense of refinement and elegance is created using negative space on the plate, enabling the eye to focus on the treat's features.

In conclusion, mastering the delicate ballet of combining culinary skill and aesthetics to create aesthetically appealing delicacies without sacrificing flavor is a must. Every component enhances the overall visual and sensory experience, from the thoughtfulness of premium ingredients to the creative plate presentation. Beyond the kitchen, the realm of culinary handicraft creates tasty artworks that stimulate the senses and make one feel happy. As we embark on this culinary adventure, let's honor the convergence of the artistic and culinary arts by producing delicacies tantalizing the senses and the sight.

CHAPTER VII

Gift-Worthy Minty Packages

Ideas for packaging and presenting cool and minty Christmas cookies as gifts

The kitchen comes alive with activity as the holidays draw near, and the smell of freshly made, minty, crisp Christmas cookies fills the air. Sharing these delicious sweets with friends, family, and loved ones is even more exciting than the joy of making them. Creating an experience that starts with the packaging and lasts until the receiver takes that first delicious bite, Christmas cookie presentation as a gift is an art form that transcends the tastes packed into each cookie. To

ensure that the happiness of giving is equal to the thrill of receiving, we use many inventive methods for packaging and presenting cool and minty Christmas cookies in this section.

A traditional cookie tin has an enduring appeal, making it the perfect container for giving Christmas cookies as gifts. Select a tin with jolly patterns, or go with one that may be customized to add a personalized touch. Line the tin with decorative tissue section or parchment section to cushion the cookies and provide an additional visual appeal. To guarantee that each cookie comes undamaged and to prevent sticking, think about stacking the cookies with sheets of wax section. For an added touch of coziness, tie a personalized gift tag to the tin and seal it with a colorful ribbon or twine.

Showcase your cold and minty Christmas cookies in mason jars for a quirky and environmentally friendly packing choice. Because of the jar's transparency, the receiver can see the cookies' layers and textures. Carefully arrange the cookies in the jar to make a pleasing arrangement. Tie some string or ribbon around the lid and fasten a tiny candy cane or a sprig of fresh mint to give it a festive touch. The mason jar provides easy storage and transportation and is a lovely packaging option.

Fill decorative cookie sacks or cartons with Christmas cookies to help you embrace the nostalgia of the season. Select boxes or bags with designs or colors related to the holidays to capture the season's essence. Line the container with parchment or tissue section to preserve the cookies and improve their appearance. Think of putting a personalized touch on the bags or boxes using stickers or labels specially printed with well-wishes for the holidays. This choice gives a portable and easy method to share your minty sweets and a gorgeous presentation.

Use ornamental tins or boxes with elaborate patterns and motifs to add a touch of refinement to your Christmas cookie display. Choose display cases with several sections to display stylish and minty cookie creations. Line the boxes with cupcake liners or parchment section for an elegant touch. Before putting the cookies in the box, dust them with powdered sugar to create a snowy effect and add to the festive atmosphere. Use a ribbon or ornamental band to close the box so the receiver can enjoy opening a well-chosen present.

Use cookie cutters with holiday themes for presentation and packaging for a fun and unique touch. Select cookie cutters with designs that remind you of the holidays, like gingerbread men, snowflakes, or Christmas trees. Cool and minty Christmas cookies should be baked right in the cookie cutters. Once cooled, carefully remove the outer shape. Use a festive ribbon to create an ornament- like display by tying it through the cookie cutter's opening. This gives the box a unique twist and functions as a two-for-one gift.

Presented in handmade packaging, Christmas cookies have an extra unique homemade feel. Make personalized cookie boxes or bags from section, beautiful wrapping section, or even recyclable materials. Embellish the package with hand-drawn images, stickers, or stamps with festive themes to give it a personalized touch. The care and attention to detail that goes into making the packaging complement the effort to make the cookies, resulting in a well-thought-out and emotional presence.
Use brown section bags or boxes tied with burlap ribbon or twine for a homey, rustic look. This packing option's simplicity lends a cozy, charming touch. Using twine or ribbon to secure, arrange the cool, minty Christmas cookies into the bags or boxes. Consider adding a cinnamon stick or fresh mint for an additional touch of Christmas scent. This option's subtle elegance highlights the handmade and sentimental quality of the gift by letting the cookies take center stage.

Tie a festive ribbon or twine loop through your minty, refreshing Christmas cookies to create tasty ornaments. Before baking, make a hole close to the edge of each cookie with a little cookie cutter. Once the cookies are cool, insert a ribbon or string through the opening and knot it firmly. For a festive appearance, bundle the cookies or arrange them in a creative arrangement. This gives your cookies a lovely touch and allows the receiver to hang them as decorations before enjoying them.

Make the most of the adaptability of cellophane or clear plastic bags to highlight the vivid hues and textures of your refreshingly minty Christmas cookies. Place the cookies in the bags so that the clear packaging shows off each one. Attach a little holiday ornament or tag to the bags for a personalized touch, then tie them with colorful ribbons or twine. This packaging option's see-through nature lets the receiver enjoy the cookies' visual beauty.

Consider making a personalized recipe booklet for holiday cookies to accompany your cold and minty Christmas cookies. Gather your most cherished recipes and kind holiday wishes, then package them with the cookies. Doing this gives the present a thoughtful touch and lets the receiver experience the enchantment of your cookies in their own kitchen. Use decorative ribbon or twine to bind the booklet and cookies together, making this a thoughtful and unforgettable gift.

Finally, the gift-giving experience is enhanced by how cool and minty Christmas cookies are packaged and presented. Every original concept provides a unique means of expressing happiness and

DIY packaging options and creative presentation ideas

Regarding gift-giving, the packaging serves as both a creative canvas and an introduction to the delight that awaits the recipient. Giving becomes an art form when you use creative presentation ideas and do-it-yourself packaging solutions to give a unique personal touch. As varied as the gifts are, the accessories can be added, from recycled materials to handmade pieces. To transform giving into a treasured experience, we will explore various do-it-yourself packaging options and creative presentation ideas in this section.

Kraft section is an excellent canvas for do-it-yourself packaging because of its earthy tones and natural texture. Take advantage of the rustic charm by decorating and packaging with kraft section. Use stencils, rubber stamps, or even hand-drawn images to create customized patterns. Burlap or twine ribbon secures the gift and allows for artistic decorations, adding a touch of rustic beauty. This straightforward but efficient strategy gives off a pleasant, homey vibe that makes the recipient eagerly anticipate receiving it. Transform regular section bags into adorable and environmentally responsible present wrapping. Adorn the bags with joyful drawings, stamps with seasonal themes, or even create collages using magazine cutouts. Using decorative washi tape, neatly fold the tops of the bags to form a border. A little decoration or a handwritten note can be fastened to the exterior to give it a personalized touch. With some imagination, the ordinary section bag may become an inventive and sustainable packaging choice.

You can use fabric as gift wrap, a sustainable and reusable packaging alternative. Select colorful designs or recycle worn-out bandanas, scarves, or fabric scraps from your sewing endeavors. Furoshiki, or fabric wrapping, is a Japanese art form that involves several sophisticated folding techniques to bind the fabric around the present. Not only does fabric gift wrap cut down on waste, but it also gives the presentation a refined look. After that, the recipient can use the cloth for other times when they want to give gifts.

Mason jars make attractive and functional wrapping for a range of presents. The options range from tiered cookie mixes to homemade jams and preserves. Attach string or ribbon to the lids after decorating them with festive fabric or section cutouts. Attach a tiny gift tag with a handwritten inscription to finish the design. The gift's visual attractiveness is enhanced by the jar's transparency, which lets the receiver see the layers and hues of the contents.

Convert outmoded books, atlases, and maps into one-of-a-kind, personalized gift wrap. Old maps have a refined and exotic look because of their complex designs and subdued hues. Use the maps to wrap gifts of different sizes and shapes by cutting them into sheets of the proper size. Add a miniature compass or travel-themed pendant to the wrapping and secure it with a contrasting ribbon or twine for an extra special touch. This do-it-yourself method not only recycles used materials but also gives the present a nostalgic feel. Create collages out of colorful pages from old catalogs, newssections, and magazines to give homemade wrapping a contemporary spin. Cut out intriguing pictures, headlines, or text, then place them on kraft or plain wrapping section. Apply decoupage adhesive to the collage pieces to create a unique, eye-catching present wrap. This method allows you to be as creative as you like and customize the collage to fit the gift's theme or the recipient's interests.

Use store-bought or hand-carved stamps to create personalized wrapping section and let your creativity run wild. Simple white or brown section rolls transform into one-of-a-kind canvases for your creative expression. Press the stamps in random or repeated patterns onto the section after dipping them in vivid ink or paint. The end product is custom wrapping section, giving the gift a unique and creative touch. Try out a variety of stamp designs to accommodate different recipients and events.

Presenting gifts stylishly and distinctively is possible with origami, the ancient Japanese art of section folding. Fold square sheets of section to create miniature origami boxes with festive colors or designs. These can contain jewelry, little trinkets, or even homemade candies. Tie a bow for decoration and tie the box with a ribbon or string. The labor-intensive construction enhances the origami box's thoughtfulness and appearance.

If wrapping an oddly shaped item is difficult, think about making a personalized gift bag out of wrapping section. Position the object at an angle on a rectangular piece of wrapping section, around it with the section, and bind the edges with tape. The size and shape of the bag can be easily customized with this straightforward method. For a last touch, add handles made of ribbon or fabric strips. Gifts of all sizes are guaranteed a personalized and eye-catching presentation when using the DIY gift bag.

Embrace a natural aspect into your gift presentation with branches, leaves, and other botanical accents. Instead of ribbon or rope, fasten twigs with a straightforward knot or bow. Attach tiny, dried flowers or leaves to the gift using glue or twine to create a lovely, natural look. This use of natural elements gives the gift a touch of rustic elegance while tying it to the splendor of the natural world.

Use personalized photo gift wrap to add a personal touch to your gift presentation. Make customized wrapping section by printing pictures of special occasions, beloved recollections, or sentimental objects.

Utilize the images to make personalized present tags or collage them onto plain wrapping section. The receiver opens a visual journey through shared memories with a thoughtful present. Giving gifts becomes more sentimental and nostalgic with this do-it-yourself alternative.

Use plain brown section bags as gift wraps for a cost-effective, vintage-inspired look. Use paint or ink to imprint graphics on the bags in a vintage style. Consider using motifs such as vintage postal stamps, elaborate keys, or detailed patterns that evoke bygone periods. This do-it-yourself method gives the gift a timeless, nostalgic charm that makes the receiver feel intrigued and eager.

In conclusion, there are a lot of opportunities to improve the art of gift-giving thanks to the universe of homemade packaging options and imaginative presentation ideas. Each method—from recycled materials to handmade embellishments—offers a unique way to bring personality and consideration to giving a gift. Whether it's the kraft section's rustic appeal,

The DIY possibilities are as varied as the inventive minds that created them, whether it's the grace of cloth wrapping or the whimsical nature of antique maps. We appreciate the delight of creating joy for others and the art of giving when we unveil ingenuity in gift wrapping.

Tips for shipping cookies to loved ones near and far

The happiness of sharing handmade cookies with loved ones transcends geographic barriers in our globalized society. Shipping cookies requires careful planning and meticulous preparation, whether you're mailing a sweet surprise to a family member in a far-off city or a batch of warm, freshly made cookies to a friend across town.

In this section, we explore the subtleties of sending these delicious treats on a journey and offer advice on ensuring the cookies arrive not only undamaged but also as a sincere token of warmth and affection.

When it comes to delivery, not all cookies are made equal. Choose robust types that maintain flavor and texture even after enduring transportation stresses. Chewy or dense cookies, such as shortbread, gingerbread, or biscotti, usually transport well. Steer clear of cookies with fragile or detailed embellishments since they could shatter or crumble en route. Choosing cookies with a robust composition lays the groundwork for a smooth delivery process.

To guarantee that they keep their structure, cookies must cool entirely before setting out on their adventure. When cookies are packed too warm, condensation may form within the container, making the finished product mushy and not tasty. Choose packaging materials that safeguard against breakage and moisture once they have cooled. To keep cookies from sticking, wrap each individually or sandwich layers of parchment section between them. Sturdy tins or containers are ideal for providing a safe and secure cookie shipping environment.

A critical factor in ensuring the safe delivery of cookies is the selection of packaging materials. Invest in sturdy, well-sized shipping boxes suitable for the number of cookies shipped. Choose robust corrugated boxes to protect against outside pressure and possible rough treatment during transit. To keep cookies from moving around and shattering, stuff any empty places in the box with packing peanuts or bubble wrap.

After the cookies are safely tucked within the container, it's imperative to seal the box. Use premium packaging tape to guarantee the package stays firmly closed during the trip. Pay close attention to strengthening the edges and seams to avoid unintentional openings during transit. Consider labeling the package with a warning that its contents are delicate so that handlers can proceed cautiously for enhanced security.

The climate of the destination significantly influences the success of exporting cookies. The quality of the goodies can be impacted by extreme heat or cold. Use cool packs or insulation to keep the cookies from melting if the weather worsens. Take precautions to prevent cookies from getting too stiff or losing their freshness in colder climates. It guarantees that the cookies arrive in optimal condition if the destination's weather is considered.

When sending cookies, timing is crucial, particularly during extraordinarily high or low temperatures. Schedule the shipping date to reduce the time the cookies spend in transit. If the cookies are being shipped to a location far from the point of origin, consider expedited shipping possibilities. By doing this, the cookies are guaranteed to travel less, lowering the likelihood of coming into contact with adverse environments. For longer trips, choose faster delivery services over standard shipping, even though the latter may be appropriate for shorter ones.

Indicate the recipient's name, address, and phone number on the package label. Include handling instructions so that shipping staff know the package's sensitive nature. Handlers can be significantly helped by a simple "Fragile" or "Handle with Care" label, which will advise them to take extra care when shipping.

Shipments become more personal when a note explaining the meaning behind the cookies and providing handling advice is placed inside the package.

Sending cookies doesn't have to be limited to using traditional delivery companies. Look into alternate delivery options that provide more individualized and cautious handling of fragile goods, like specialty food shipping firms or local courier services. Several services are created to guarantee that the cookies arrive in the best possible condition, especially for delivering perishable items, and can offer temperature-controlled facilities.

Remember to value a human touch; it goes beyond packaging and delivery logistics. A passionate card or message detailing the present's contents and expressing your feelings should be included. Think of having a personal note about the cookies, like the recipe or a backstory. This creates a shared experience around receiving cookies and strengthening the emotional bond.

Use the tracking options shipping companies provide to monitor the package's progress. The shipper and the recipient can feel more at ease knowing that the shipment is being tracked and receiving real-time updates on its position and progress. To further guarantee that the intended receiver receives the cookies, request delivery confirmation or require a signature upon receipt.
Provide advice on how to store the cookies after they arrive. Whether they should be eaten right once or put in the freezer or fridge to be consumed later

When consuming, precise instructions guarantee that the receiver can enjoy the sweets at their peak freshness. Providing storage advice shows consideration and enhances the overall satisfaction of receiving and savoring the supplied cookies.

In conclusion, sending cookies to family members who live far away is a skill that blends thoughtful gestures with realistic considerations. Senders may guarantee a delightful and successful journey by picking the perfect cookies, chilling and wrapping them appropriately, selecting suitable packaging materials, and considering the destination climate. Timing, shipping choices, labeling, and handling instructions all help ensure the cookies arrive safely, and adding a personal touch gives the present more coziness and significance. When these suggestions are carefully followed, sending cookies may become a thoughtful and tasty experience for both the sender and the fortunate recipient, regardless of how far the cookies must travel.

CHAPTER VIII

Hosting a Minty Cookie Exchange

Planning and organizing a successful cool and minty cookie exchange party

There are many fun activities during the holidays, and one cute custom that perfectly embodies sweetness and sharing is the cookie exchange party. The chilly and minty cookie exchange stands out as a distinctive and revitalizing take on the traditional cookie swap as friends and family get together to celebrate. To guarantee a smooth and joyful experience for every attendee, meticulous planning and attention to detail are essential when organizing an event of this kind. To understand the vital components that add to the enchantment of this chilly event, we will design and execute a cold and minty cookie exchange party in this section.

Securing a cool and minty cookie exchange celebration starts with carefully choosing the location. Think about an area that promotes a joyful environment, lots of seats, and easy interaction. The location creates the mood for the joyous occasion, whether it's the large kitchen with a scent of minty treats or the comfortable living area with twinkling lights. Ensure the event's location can hold the number of attendees and create a warm, inviting atmosphere for the minty and chilly motif.

Creating the ideal invites sets the tone for the sophisticated, minty celebration. Try experimenting with winter-themed designs using icy blue and green tones, or add whimsy snowflakes and mint leaves. Ensure everyone understands the cookie exchange's theme and is inspired to create cookies that embody the refreshing and minty vibe. Ideas like "Winter Wonderland" or "Minty Magic" give guests an imaginative framework and build excitement for the occasion.

Provide precise instructions for the cookies to provide a varied and tasty selection. Give participants instructions on how to enjoy the cold, minty flavor profile and encourage them to try spearmint, peppermint, or other cooling variations. Give samples of traditional minty treats to stimulate creativity, such as chocolate mint cookies, peppermint bark cookies, or mint chocolate chip cookies. Decide on a sensible amount each person can bring to allow variation without overwhelming those who contribute. Provide a sign-up sheet or online form where participants may select the cookie they like, avoiding duplication and guaranteeing a varied assortment. Include excellent, refreshing items in the décor to turn the space into a minty wonderland. Combine mint green, frosty blue, and crisp white to create a wintry atmosphere. Arrange centerpieces with twigs, snowflakes, and fresh mint leaves to further the idea. To add a whimsical touch, think about hanging decorations that mimic mint candies or strung fairy lights. All guests should have an immersive experience as the relaxed, minty vibe permeates the setting.

Provide a dedicated display area to bring the calm presentation of minty biscuits to the next level. Arrange each participant's work on a table with festive trays, cake stands, or elegant platters. Request that volunteers provide cookies in containers with coordinating themes, including boxes colored mint, bags decorated with snowflakes, or jars tied with bows mint. In addition to being a culinary treat, the cookie exchange is visually appealing and enriches the whole experience.

Serve cool drinks and nibbles with the minty, refreshing cookies. Set up a hot chocolate station with crushed candy canes, whipped cream, and syrups with mint flavors for a luxurious touch. A distinctive minty drink, iced peppermint lattes, or even teas laced with mint can elevate the occasion. To counterbalance the sweetness of the cookies, think of serving palate-cleansing options like fresh fruit platters or a refreshing mint sorbet. Incorporate interactive entertainment and activities to enhance the celebratory atmosphere further. Make a refreshing playlist of Christmas favorites or music with a winter vibe. Please set up a cookie decorating station with various minty toppings to let guests personalize their cookies. Include a game with a cookie theme or a festive photo booth with minty-cool decorations for extra fun. These activities add to the enjoyment and produce priceless memories for everyone involved.

You can introduce a pleasant competitive element by including a judging component in the cookie exchange. Establish award categories like "Best Presentation," "Most Creative," or "Mintiest Flavor" to recognize and honor the contributions of participants. To choose the winners, ask guests to vote or select a panel of judges. To acknowledge the contributions of individuals who excel in various categories, consider providing diplomas or minor incentives. This makes the conversation more lighthearted and motivates attendees to give it their all. Give them takeaways and favors to carry the refreshing and minty motif after the event. Give each guest a tiny packet of mint candies, a candle with a peppermint smell, or a specially prepared minty lip balm. Not only can these tokens show appreciation for their involvement, but they also function as keepsakes from the chilly event. Personalized recipe cards with a minty theme that highlights the provided cookies are thoughtful additions that guarantee the minty, relaxed vibe will last.

Take pictures of the occasion to capture the magic of the refreshing cookie exchange. Please set up a photo area with festive backdrops and props so that guests can take pictures of themselves. Assign a photographer or urge attendees to hashtag the event when posting their photos on social media. Gather the images and make a physical scrapbook or digital album to preserve the memories of the refreshing party. This helps keep the event going and brings back happy memories for the participants.

In conclusion, creating a relaxed and minty cookie exchange party requires a complex tapestry of original ideas and well-considered details. Every element of the event, from arranging a varied selection of minty treats to creating a wintry scene on the stage, adds to its overall success. Cool and minty cookie exchange becomes more than just a food exchange; it becomes a treasured custom that warms hearts and leaves enduring memories for everyone who participates in the frosty occasion by bringing a sense of community, creativity, and festive spirit to the gathering.

Invitations, decorations, and activities to make the event memorable

A memorable event requires a carefully balanced act of imagination, careful preparation, and a hint of magic. A special event may be created with the perfect combination of invites, décor, and activities—whether for a birthday celebration, holiday get-together, or other special occasion. This section delves into the nuances of creating a genuinely unforgettable event. It looks at the skill of creating invites that arouse interest, décor that captivates the senses, and activities that include and excite guests.

The art of invitation goes beyond simply communicating the specifics of the event; it's a preamble to what's to come. The first stage in building anticipation is to create invitations that are both visually arresting and informative. Whether the event is a classy gala, a whimsical garden party, or a fun celebration for all ages, pick a theme that captures the spirit of the occasion. Use theme-related design components, color schemes, and imagery to give guests a preview of the mood they might expect. Add individualized details to every invitation, including the guest's name, to make them feel unique. Use multimedia components or interactive features in your digital invitations to up the ante. The intention is to create a memorable event by arousing curiosity and enthusiasm from the minute the invitation is received.

The potential of decorations to immerse guests in a new world and improve the entire experience gives them their transforming power. Coordinating decorations with the theme is essential to create a unified and enchanted atmosphere at the location. Think about how lighting affects the room because it can drastically change the atmosphere. A warm and welcoming glow can be added with string lights, candles, or LED installations; different colored lighting can create different feelings. Try layering richly colored textiles for a formal event or adding fun patterns for a more laid-back get-together to create depth by experimenting with textures and materials. Table arrangements, centerpieces, and the thoughtful arrangement of these components add to the eye-catching visual feast that draws guests in. The location should be transformed into a canvas of memories ready to be painted with decorations that weave a narrative that matches the event's theme, whether personalized banners, hanging ornaments, or floral arrangements.

The activities that captivate, amuse, and make an impression on guests are the lifeblood of a memorable event. A carefully chosen program of activities guarantees that the event is more than just a get-together—it's an adventure, from conversation starters that encourage interaction to multisensory experiences that stimulate the senses. Adapt activities to the audience's inclinations and demographics. Consider using team-building activities that promote cooperation and friendship for a business gathering. All ages can be entertained in a family celebration with interactive games, craft stations, and scavenger hunts. Activities with a theme that fits the event's story improve overall cohesion and leave a lasting impression. Incorporate aspects of surprise, such as interactive displays, live entertainment, or surprising performances. Finding the right mix between planned events and unplanned opportunities for people to bond and make memories is crucial naturally.

The natural charm of a memorable event is when invitations, decorations, and activities work together harmoniously. There's a smooth transition from expectation to immersion since the decorations carry over the theme presented in the invitation. Consider a retro-themed party with invites that have tasteful typography and sepia-toned photos. Visitors are welcomed into a space with elegant lighting, antique décor, and a jazz band performing music from bygone eras. The events could be a swing dance lesson floor and a vintage prop-filled picture booth. The seamless experience weaves a tale, ensuring that each component contributes to the plot, from the first invitation to the last task. This balance turns the occasion from a collection of disparate elements into a symphony of sensations that guests remember long after the festivities.

A genuinely remarkable occasion is characterized by customizing every component, including the activities, decorations, and invitations. Consider the participants' backgrounds, interests, and preferences when creating invitations. Incorporating inside jokes or experiences shared with the guest of honor or customizing the design to showcase their preferred colors or pastimes are examples of personal touches. Add sentimental or evocative elements to your decorations to further extend this personalizing. Modifying activities to better suit the audience's interests is also possible. These carefully considered touches take the event from generic to truly meaningful, whether a tailored playlist reflecting a range of musical likes or a trivia game with questions about the attendees' past. When attendees feel seen, valued, and part of the story, they are more likely to remember the event.

Not only can large gestures make an occasion memorable, but flawless execution of every detail does as well. Attend to the invites' logistics, ensuring they are sent out well in advance and contain all pertinent information. The arrangement of the decorations should improve the event's flow and take guests on a visual tour. Clear directions, backup plans, and a well-planned schedule should all be present during activities. Attendees may concentrate entirely on the experience at a well-run event, free from interruptions caused by unplanned technical difficulties. Attendees are left with a favorable impression that lasts a long time when an event is executed with professionalism and attention to detail.

Events are fleeting, emphasizing how crucial it is to record memories that guests can keep. To capture the event, spend money on expert photography or videography services. The happy moments are captured in candid, group, and action images taken at events. To enable attendees to bring tangible souvenirs home, think of erecting a unique photo booth complete with themed props. Include a designated photo-sharing platform or a social media hashtag to encourage guests to share their viewpoints. Attendees can explore and relive the magic any time they'd like, thanks to the tangible legacy that the preserved memories provide. In conclusion, the delicate tango between invitations, decorations, and activities is the key to creating an event that will be remembered. Invitations open the door to anticipation; decorations turn the space into a sensory paradise, and activities weave the experiences together to build the unique fabric of the occasion. When these components come together, driven by customization, careful planning, and flawless execution, the event goes above and beyond the norm. It leaves a lasting impression on the minds and hearts of those who attended. Ultimately, a genuinely unforgettable event is more than simply a one-time occurrence; it's a trip, an experience, and a compilation of moments that will be remembered for years.

Sharing the joy of holiday baking with friends and family

Around the world, kitchens undergo a mystical metamorphosis as the holiday season approaches. Countertops are dusted with flour, the air is filled with the aroma of nutmeg and cinnamon, and the oven's warmth becomes a ray of consolation. This metamorphosis is nothing more than the beloved custom of baking over the holidays. This ritual unites the themes of love, community, and joy while going beyond recipes and ingredients. This section explores the significance of the holiday baking custom that extends beyond the delicious goods that come out of the oven and the delightful experience of sharing the joy of baking with friends and family.

Baking for the holidays is a social activity that builds relationships rather than being a solo endeavor. Whether with parents, siblings, or close friends, gathering in the kitchen creates a common area for jokes, chatter, and sharing tales. Across generations, the kitchen becomes a center of shared history and nostalgia as family members gather to cook up beloved recipes or try new culinary endeavors. Individuals add to a communal memory by measuring, mixing, and baking rhythmically, passing down customs that endure over time. The ability of shared traditions to strengthen friendships and family bonds is demonstrated by holiday baking, which weaves a richer web of connection with every year that goes by.

Holiday baking provides an opportunity for creativity and experimentation, and the season inspires gastronomic inquiry. The choices are endless, matching the imagination of those using the spatulas. The options are endless, from traditional favorites like fruitcakes and gingerbread cookies to contemporary takes like peppermint bark brownies or eggnog-flavored cupcakes. The kitchen becomes a playground where people experiment with flavors and create new customs. Baking becomes an art form as friends and family work together to create one-of-a-kind sweets and go on extraordinary culinary adventures. The Christmas season is exciting by the spirit of inventiveness and the delight of discovery, which transforms every collaborative baking session into a taste experience to be cherished.

In baking for the holidays, recipes take on the significance of family history and are cherished relics. These recipes, passed down from grandparents to parents and subsequently to kids, are a physical connection to the past rather than merely a list of ingredients. A cherished family recipe can be recreated as a moving homage to the past and a method to preserve the culinary legacy that has influenced family customs. Whether it's the trick ingredient in Grandma's sugar cookies or the exact process in Dad's well-known pumpkin pie, these recipes hold stories of love, resiliency, and the eternal spirit of celebration.

Baking during the holidays is a sensory symphony that appeals to the senses of smell, touch, sight, and taste. When the scent of warm, spiced cake or freshly made cookies fills the air, it acts as a beacon, announcing the start of the holiday season. Hands are engaged in a creative dance when kneading dough, rolling out pie crusts, and decorating gingerbread houses. A dimension of artistry is added to the experience by the visual attractiveness of a dessert that has been expertly presented or a tray of cookies that has been carefully decorated. Holiday baking weaves a sensory tapestry that accentuates the excitement of the occasion and provides a memorable multisensory experience that lasts long after the last cookie is consumed.

Baking for the holidays offers a chance for culinary instruction in addition to indulgence. The holidays turn into a classroom where experienced bakers impart their wisdom to those new to the kitchen. Grandparents share their pie crust secrets, parents teach their kids how to measure ingredients, and friends trade tips for making the perfect cookie texture. During holiday baking sessions, transferring culinary expertise to others is a mentorship that transcends the kitchen. It gives people self-assurance, encourages a love of cooking, and allows them to carry the legacy proudly. Baking for the holidays becomes an ongoing educational process and a never-ending gift.

The results of Christmas baking are meant to be shared with others in addition to the people gathering around the kitchen table. Baked goods turn into palatable expressions of affection and thoughtfulness, ideal for giving as gifts to friends, family, coworkers, or anyone particularly dear to oneself. Giving someone a festive loaf of bread or a beautifully wrapped box of baked cookies is a gesture that is more meaningful than money can buy. It represents the work, energy, and attention to detail that makes something unique for someone else. The sincerity of a homemade dessert speaks volumes in a world full of commercialism; it carries the emotion of shared joy and the warmth of the season.

Holiday baking promotes inclusion and unity by acting as a common language that cuts across cultural and religious divides. Even though different households may have other recipes, making and sharing holiday snacks is universal. The underlying attitude is celebration, giving, and community, whether baked into Christmas cookies in the United States, Stollen in Germany, or Basbousa in Egypt. When individuals from diverse cultures get together for a shared event that celebrates variety and emphasizes the universal thread of human connection, holiday baking serves as a bridge.

When it comes to holiday baking, the authenticity of the finished product and the joy of the process take precedence over precision. Unexpected twists and baking disasters are woven into the story, giving it a lighthearted and humble feel. The slightly over-browned crust, the collapsed soufflé, or the imperfectly shaped cookies are not failures but honors that attest to the capricious character of Christmas baking. Accepting imperfection becomes a potent resilience and adaptability lesson that reminds participants that the delight is not in perfect results but in creating something together.

For many who bake during the holidays, the memories made during the baking process are just as memorable as the baked goods as the season ends. The intangibles create the foundation of enduring memories: the patient guidance throughout the learning moments, the aroma filling the kitchen, and the laughter shared when rolling out dough. Many years later, someone can be sent back in time to the warmth of their kitchen, surrounded by loved ones, creating holiday treats just by mentioning a particular recipe or inhaling the aroma of a comforting spice. These deeply ingrained memories serve as a source of solace, nostalgia, and a constant reminder of the lasting value of shared experiences.

In summary, the pleasure of baking for the holidays extends beyond the kitchen and into the domains of tradition, connection, and shared experiences. It's a custom that turns common ingredients into unforgettable memories and celebrates love, creativity, and community. Around mixing basins and ovens, families and friends congregate.

Individuals participate in a timeless custom that yields delicious delicacies and stitches together enduring bonds and priceless memories. The delight of baking during the holidays is a heartfelt celebration. This delightful symphony captures the essence of the occasion and leaves a legacy of warmth and affection for future generations.

CHAPTER IX

Memories and Traditions

Reflecting on the role of cool and minty cookies in creating holiday memories

Certain flavors stand out as the fundamental components of this enchanted time of year as the holiday season unfolds its joyful tapestry. The distinct flavor of mint stands out among cinnamon, ginger, and chocolate aromas. It is a refreshing and excellent alternative. Holiday lovers have a special place in their hearts and mouths for cool, minty cookies that are so delightful. This section takes the reader on a contemplative trip as we examine how these delicious sweets contribute to making holiday memories and the connections that bind them to our most treasured customs.

The bright blend of flavors in these cool and minty biscuits creates a sensory symphony that perfectly captures the spirit of the holiday. The cookie's sweetness combines with spearmint or peppermint's cooling effect to create a harmonious flavor that tingles the palate. It's a gastronomic dance in which every mouthful is a step into a wintry wonderland, a brief sojourn in a realm infused with the flavor of mint. Beyond taste, the perfume of mint fills the kitchen while baking, infusing the air with a crisp scent instantly associated with festive cheer. Cool and minty cookies become a sensory bridge that links us to the wonder of the holidays, adding to the general ambiance of the season and the feast on the table.

A time for nostalgia abounds during the holidays, and chilly, minty cookies act as doors to priceless memories. Many people associate peppermint with warm evenings by the fire, special occasions with loved ones, and the excitement of opening holiday goodies. Making cookies or enjoying cool, minty treats turns into a multigenerational rite. A legacy of memories that span generations is created when parents revive old favorites, grandparents share recipes, and kids enthusiastically participate in the custom. Every mouthful carries a hint of nostalgia, a delightful remembrance of previous holidays, and the timeless happiness that comes from comforting tastes.

The appeal of these refreshingly minty cookies is their ability to be creative while staying true to tradition. Some people stick to traditional recipes, such as peppermint bark cookies or candies inspired by candy canes. Still, others take a creative approach to cooking and incorporate mint into unique dishes like chocolate mint thumbprints or shortbread with mint. Cool, minty cookies are ageless and versatile because of the ingredient's malleability, which encourages flavor experimentation. This adaptability is evidence of how holiday customs constantly change, fusing the traditional with the modern to create a delicious spread that suits a wide range of tastes.

Cool, minty cookies provide a welcome break from the rich and sumptuous selection of holiday goodies. The cold, refreshing aromas of mint balance off the intensity of chocolate, the sweetness of caramel, and the buttery richness of classic cookies. On the holiday dessert table, this contrast produces a pleasing balance that enables people to enjoy a range of flavors without becoming overwhelmed. Crisp, minty cookies act as a palette cleanser, a little break that revitalizes the palate and provides a refreshing diversion from the season's overindulgent heat.

Making crisp, minty cookies for the holidays is more than just a cooking project—it's an artistic statement. Bakers are encouraged to explore hues, forms, and seasonal accents to capture the season's essence by using the festive subject of mint. Imagine the process: mixing the dough, adding the mint extract, watching the cookies bake in the oven, and finally, decorating them with festive flourishes. The presentation of cool and minty biscuits takes on hues ranging from vivid green to delicate swirls reminiscent of candy cane. From amateurs to seasoned lovers, baking is a joyful process when essential ingredients are transformed into edible artwork reflecting the holidays' visual magic. Cool and minty cookie decorating becomes a way to express yourself festively and allows you to add your unique style and inventiveness to each batch.

Cool and minty cookies have a unique power to bring people together and build a sense of friendship. Whether they are made as a family project, shared as a token of friendship, or traded among friends, these sweets serve as a means of fostering relationships. Beyond sharing food, passing along a tray of crisp, minty cookies is a sign of kindness and an "I thought of you." Eating these cookies together creates a community experience that heals wounds, builds relationships, and increases the cheerfulness of the holidays. Cool and minty cookies foster moments of connection that stay in the hearts of individuals who indulge in their sweetness in a world where things frequently move quickly.

The comfort of tradition is significant during the holidays in the ever-changing environment of modern life. Crisp, minty cookies symbolize comfort when they remain a constant fixture on the dessert table. They represent tradition's consistency, providing stability in a world of change. Baking or indulging in chilly, minty cookies is a way to reconnect with the essence of Christmas festivities —a reassuring hug that lasts beyond the fleeting passage of time. The comforting familiarity of mint is a constant reminder that certain things haven't altered much throughout the years.

Cool and minty cookies play a particular part in the big symphony of seasonal flavors—a trademark note that gives the composition depth and subtlety. The seamless blending of each distinct component defines the symphony rather than just the individual instruments. Refreshing music paired with excellent, minty cookies adds to the festive experience's richness. These cookies become essential to the holiday soundtrack, producing a sensory mosaic that uplifts the season's spirit, whether eaten with hot chocolate, shared during festive parties, or savored in quiet introspection.

In summary, minty, cool cookies are more than just treats—they're messengers of happiness, fond memories, and kinship. When we consider how these goodies contribute to making holiday memories, we realize that they are more than just delicious foods; they appeal to our senses and become ingrained in our most treasured customs. Every mouthful tells a tale of get-togethers with family and friends, artistic pursuits, and intimate moments. A symphony of memories that reverberate over time is created by the cool, minty cookies, with their refreshing charm, acting as ambassadors of the holiday spirit.

Collecting and preserving family recipes and traditions

Every family has a culinary tapestry woven with strands of shared ancestry, love, and tradition at its core. Family recipes are a treasured repository of memories and relationships passed down through the generations, in addition to being a set of cooking instructions. In this section, we examine the profound significance of gathering and conserving family recipes and customs, realizing that they are the glue that unites generations and the cornerstone upon which a family's identity is constructed.

Family recipes are time capsules that capture the spirit of a bygone age; they are more than just cooking instructions. Every dish is a window into the past, providing a flavor profile that shaped the family's past. These food relics hold stories of resiliency, celebration, and daily living, from the beloved apple pie recipe Grandma mastered in the 1950s to the hearty stew that saw generations through difficult times. Preserving family recipes means protecting a legacy—a material link to the events, victories, and difficulties that molded the family's path through time.

Families protect their culinary legacy and identity in addition to various meals by collecting and preserving family recipes. Every recipe serves as a brushstroke on the family's cultural canvas, capturing local flavors, customs, and the distinct culinary tastes of the past. Family recipes represent an artistic fingerprint, a mark that sets one family's culinary identity apart from another, whether it's the family recipe passed down through the years, or the ingredient kept hidden in Great-Grandmother's sauce. Preserving these recipes is a deliberate endeavor to uphold continuity and transmit a rich cultural legacy to the following generation.

Family recipes serve as a link between generations, bridging the past and present and the future. A generational conversation occurs when grandparents impart their culinary knowledge to their grandkids. The kitchen turns into a classroom, and recipes serve as textbooks that teach culinary skills and the ancestors' morals, anecdotes, and knowledge. This conversation acknowledges the cyclical cycle of life and the importance of food in keeping families together as the tides change. Intentionally creating these generational connections through gathering and preserving family recipes ensures that the traditions and wisdom are passed down year after year.

Family recipes are the live expressions of customs; each flavor serves as a thread that ties together the various aspects of familial traditions. These recipes are the keepers of tradition, from the joyous meal that adorns the table during holiday get-togethers to the regular comfort food that provides comfort in difficult times. Making and serving these foods becomes a ritual that concretely expresses cultural norms and shared values. The flavors that dance on the tongue and the scents that fill the kitchen become the language used to celebrate and transmit traditions. Thus, keeping family recipes represents a dedication to maintaining the cultural fabric that shapes a family's distinct character.

Familiar flavors have an emotional solid resonance that defies space and time. Family recipes have an incredible power to bring people back to special times, arouse feelings, and return them to memories. A dish cooked just the way mom used to make it can transport you back to your carefree days, and the smell of a particular spice can bring back memories of get-togethers with loved ones and joyous occasions. By gathering and conserving family recipes, families preserve the cooking instructions and the emotional essence that imbues such foods with a lasting place in their collective recollections. The comfort that comes from the flavor of a well-known recipe is evidence of the food's continuing ability to serve as a medium for fostering emotional bonds.

A deliberate investment in strengthening family ties is the gathering and preservation of family recipes. These culinary rituals, which can include anything from the weekly family meal showcasing a signature dish to the annual practice of baking cookies together, promote a sense of community and shared experience. These traditions serve as anchors to keep families rooted in the here and now in a world when time frequently appears to be slipping away. A family's bond is strengthened by the times spent together, such as the laughter reverberating through the kitchen during a cooking session or the shared delight of making a cherished recipe.

Family recipes take on the role of time capsules, commemorating significant events and years gone by. Birthdays could be celebrated by unveiling a particular cake recipe, anniversaries with the making of a secret sauce, and holiday feasts with foods served for generations. Family recipes provide a feeling of continuity and legacy by acting as checkpoints throughout a family's life cycle. Reading over these recipes again becomes a way to honor the past, celebrate the present, and look forward to the future with a sense of purpose as new chapters are written.

Gathering and conserving family recipes is an obligation to the past and a promise to the coming generations.

Preserving family recipes becomes a way to ensure that the roots stay in place in a world that is changing quickly, where cultural landscapes and traditional behaviors change. It's an investment in the cultural education of future generations of family members, giving them a guide to navigating their ancestry and a sense of the tastes that characterize their lineage. Recipients are offering the following generation the responsibility of looking after their family's culinary legacy when they pass along recipes.

Family recipes are a testament to history but lend themselves to change and adaptation. Family recipes are dynamic and, like living things, can change somewhat to accommodate evolving tastes and Inclinations. The realization that family recipes are dynamic and that each generation adds to the continuing story is what makes gathering and conserving family recipes so beautiful. Family members add layers to the unfolding narrative of the family's culinary adventure as they play with changes or add new ingredients to traditional recipes. The adaptability of preserving family recipes ensures that customs live on and are meaningfully connected to every generation.

Gathering and archiving family recipes goes beyond the family unit and touches on shared cultural experiences and the community. Families participate in broader cross-cultural exchanges when they share recipes with friends, neighbors, and other family members. Families in a community can bond through the everyday experience of making and savoring these dishes, which promotes a sense of identity and shared history. Preserving family recipes becomes a cooperative endeavor that enhances the more significant cultural fabric by assembling a mosaic of many culinary customs that mix and mingle.

To sum up, gathering and conserving family recipes is an intricate and meaningful process. It is a dedication to preserving the tastes, customs, and memories that characterize a family's identity. Families build a timeless continuity that spans generations, linking the past with the present and the present with the future by preserving these culinary treasures. Family recipes are the threads that bind together families, define cultural identities, and create a tapestry of shared experiences that are cherished and timeless. Gathering and conserving family recipes celebrates love, connection, and the rich tapestry of human experience in the kitchen, where fragrances linger and traditions are stirred into reality.

Encouraging readers to create their own Christmas cookie traditions

Christmas cookies are a distinctive and beloved custom many people hold dear as the holiday season envelops us in its magical embrace. Christmas cookies are the epitome of coziness, happiness, and the feeling of community—not to mention how good they taste. We invite readers to build and embrace their own Christmas cookie traditions and enjoy the deliciousness of holiday cookies as we set off on a path of encouragement in this section. These customs, infused with unique elements and familial flare, can change the Christmas season into a period of joyous celebration, enduring memories, and the establishment of treasured rituals.

The essence of tradition—a celebration of continuity, connection, and the passing down of shared experiences—lies at the core of Christmas cookie customs. You are engaging in a timeless tradition beyond the kitchen by starting your Christmas cookie traditions. It's a chance to connect to the past by creating new memories or taking inspiration from holiday cookie customs passed down through the centuries. Acknowledging the significance of these modest yet profound actions that characterize the holiday season is essential to embracing the core of tradition.

Making your own Christmas cookie customs is a kind of alchemy, a captivating fusion of culinary skill, inventiveness, and the season's romance. It's an invitation to explore flavors, forms, and decorations that speak to your style and enter the kitchen with a sense of wonder and possibility. Beyond just following a recipe, baking Christmas cookies is an artistic endeavor, a window into one's palate, and a chance to imbue every batch with the warmth and cheer that define the season.

Your unique touches and personalization are what make your Christmas cookie tradition memorable. The process becomes an extension of your personality and tastes, whether it's the usage of unique ingredient combinations, cherished family recipes, or inventive flavor combinations. Think about adding nostalgic flavors to your cookies to make them seem more reflective, or use your decorating imagination to give each cookie a special touch only you can provide. Putting your personal touch on your Christmas cookies turns them from culinary representations of you to a secret ritual.

When Christmas cookie traditions are created and shared with loved ones, they are more significant. Baking becomes a community activity when friends, family, or neighbors participate; it's a shared experience promoting unity and connection. Consider throwing a cookie decorating party where guests can bring their best recipes or work together to create something new. The shared laughs, stories, and cooperative work make the ritual more joyful, which fosters a sense of oneness that permeates the entire holiday celebration, not just in the kitchen.

Christmas cookies can convey tales of custom, history, and individual experiences. As you craft your customs around Christmas cookies, consider the stories you want to tell with the food. Maybe it's the tale of a grandma's cookie recipe, the story of a unique ingredient with family history, or the story of a brand-new recipe that opens a new chapter in your family's holiday traditions. The custom gains complexity from the culinary storytelling, which transforms each batch of cookies into a chapter in the book of your family's holiday story. Traditions around Christmas cookies are about more than just enjoying delicious treats—they're also about encapsulating the giving spirit. If your ritual includes gift-giving, consider baking additional loaves for neighbors, friends, or those in need. Spread the joy of your Christmas cookie tradition to others, gift the cookies in festive containers, and personalize them with handwritten notes. Giving grows in importance as part of the custom, generating a chain reaction of goodwill and providing that captures the genuine spirit of the occasion.

Developing your customs for Christmas cookies adds a sense of routine and rhythm to the occasion. Every stage of the process, from selecting which recipes to bake to the joyous decorating ritual, becomes a part of a giant dance that mimics the rhythm of the Christmas season. In contrast to the hectic pace of holiday preparations, these seasonal traditions provide a feeling of order and expectation. Participating in these rhythmic customs is a stabilizing factor that enables you to appreciate and absorb entirely the splendor of the Christmas season.

Making enduring memories may be the most alluring part of starting your Christmas cookie customs. The sound of laughing and the aroma of freshly baked cookies fill the kitchen, setting the scene for memories that stay with everyone involved. These memories, which range from the happy commotion of a family cookie decorating party to the reflective moments when you relish the first taste of a freshly baked cookie, become woven into the fabric of your life.

Recollections of the holidays. Establishing traditions involves more than just enjoying the here and now; it also entails creating a storehouse of special memories that will be recalled and appreciated for years.

Making your Christmas cookie customs is lovely because they are flexible and can change with time. Your cookie customs can adapt and grow with you as life changes. Seize the chance to add fresh ingredients, try out other recipes, or alter classics to accommodate changing inclinations and tastes. Your cookie traditions are flexible enough to keep them interesting, novel, and relevant to the stage of life you're in at the moment. This allows for the steady development of a custom that is both ageless and active.

As you enjoy making Christmas cookie traditions, think about how important it is to record and preserve the recipes and anecdotes that go along with them. Make a digital archive or recipe diary for the holidays where you may record the additions and changes you make every year. This gives your tradition an extra layer of structure and turns it into a priceless heirloom you can pass on to the next generations. The recording is a deliberate attempt to guarantee that the tales and formulas that characterize your distinct Christmas cookie custom are conserved and transmitted to future generations.

To summarize, starting your Christmas cookie customs is a call to pursue a path filled with joy, creativity, and connection. It honors the distinct tastes, individualized touches, and communal moments that contribute to the enchantment of the holiday season. You are not merely making cookies when you imbue your customs with love, coziness, and the feeling of community; instead, you are establishing a legacy that will be a source of happiness, kinship, and the delightful symphony of your family's distinct holiday story. Thus, this Christmas, let the aroma of freshly made cookies fill your house like music and let the process of making your own unique Christmas cookie customs serve as a touching theme that will last for years.

CONCLUSION

Summing up the joy of baking cool and minty Christmas cookies

The holiday season brings a sense of warmth and joy, filling the air with the sweet aroma of festive treats. Among the myriad delights that grace our tables during this time, Christmas cookies hold a special place, and there's a particular magic in baking cool and minty variations. Baking becomes a cherished tradition, connecting generations and creating memories that linger long after the last cookie is savored.

The kitchen becomes a haven of warmth and activity as the winter chill sets in. Gathering ingredients - flour, sugar, eggs, butter, and, of course, the show's star, mint - brings a sense of anticipation. Baking cool and minty Christmas cookies is not just about creating delicious treats; it's a journey through time and tradition. The mixer's rhythmic whir, vanilla wafting through the air, and the vibrant green of the mint-infused dough evoke a sensory symphony that encapsulates the season's spirit.

The choice of mint in Christmas cookies introduces a refreshing twist, cutting through the sweetness with an excellent and refreshing flavor. With its association with winter and freshness, the Mint symbolizes renewal and celebration. Each cutout shape becomes a canvas for creativity as the dough is rolled out. The transformation from a simple mixture to a tray of intricately shaped cookies is a testament to the artistry of the holiday baking tradition.

The oven becomes a portal, bridging the gap between raw ingredients and the final product. The alchemy that occurs within its heated confines is nothing short of magical. The once pliable dough transforms into golden- brown masterpieces, filling the kitchen with an irresistible aroma that beckons even the most reluctant taste buds. The joy of watching cookies rise and spread, taking on their final form, is a reward in itself - a tangible manifestation of the love and effort invested in the baking process.

As the cookies cool on wire racks, their minty fragrance permeates the kitchen, signaling the imminent joy that awaits. Frosting or drizzling chocolate over the cooled cookies adds an extra layer of artistry. Each stroke of frosting becomes a personal touch, a signature distinguishing one batch from another. The minty freshness mingles with the sweetness of the frosting, creating a harmonious balance that tantalizes the taste buds.

Beyond the delightful taste and aroma, sharing these incredible and minty Christmas cookies is a gesture of love and generosity. The tradition of gifting homemade treats is a universal language that transcends cultural boundaries. A box of carefully crafted cookies becomes a token of appreciation, expressing warmth and goodwill during the festive season. Relationships are strengthened by exchanging these edible gifts, and a sense of community is fostered.

Moreover, baking cool and minty Christmas cookies is an educational journey, especially for younger generations. Children, with their wide-eyed wonder, learn the art of measurement, mixing, and patience. The kitchen becomes a classroom where valuable life skills are imparted in the guise of a joyous activity. The passing down of family recipes, handed down through generations, becomes a tangible link to the past, creating a sense of continuity and heritage.

The calm and minty Christmas cookies, with their vibrant colors and distinct flavors, also become a centerpiece for holiday gatherings. They adorn dessert tables, inviting guests to enjoy a sensory experience beyond taste. Biting into a minty cookie becomes a shared moment of delight, a communal appreciation for the efforts put into creating something unique. The cookies, arranged in festive patterns, become a visual feast that adds to the overall ambiance of the holiday celebration.

In a world that often seems to move frenetically, baking cool and minty Christmas cookies introduces a pause, a moment of reflection and connection. The kitchen, with its flour-dusted surfaces and the hum of the oven, becomes a sanctuary where individuals come together to create something beautiful. The shared laughter, the exchange of stories, and the collaborative effort required in baking foster bonds beyond the final product.

In conclusion, the joy of baking cool and minty Christmas cookies is not confined to the delectable taste or the festive aesthetics. It is a holistic experience encompassing tradition, creativity, generosity, and connection. With its mixers and ovens, the kitchen becomes a portal to a world where time seems to slow down, allowing individuals to savor the process and each other's company. As the cookies are shared and enjoyed, the true essence of the holiday season is encapsulated in these sweet, mint-infused creations, bringing joy to both the bakers and those fortunate enough to indulge in the fruits of their labor.

Encouraging readers to continue experimenting with flavors and creating new Traditions

In the realm of culinary exploration, a rich tapestry of flavors is waiting to be discovered, and traditions are yet to be woven. As the world becomes more interconnected, the fusion of diverse culinary traditions opens up a playground for experimentation. Encouraging readers to embark on this gastronomic journey is not merely a call to spice up their kitchens; it's an invitation to forge new traditions, breathing life into the age-old art of cooking.

Experimenting with flavors is akin to an artist dabbling with an expansive palette. Just as a painter mixes and blends colors to create a masterpiece, a chef combines various tastes and textures to craft culinary wonders. The allure of experimenting lies not only in the novelty of the results but in the process itself—a creative dance with ingredients that sparks innovation and surprises the taste buds. Readers are encouraged to break free from the shackles of culinary routine and embrace the joyous chaos of flavor exploration.

This culinary odyssey begins with a departure from the familiar and a willingness to embrace the unknown. It's about infusing a pinch of boldness into the mundane, turning the ordinary into the extraordinary. Whether it's the marriage of contrasting flavors or the fusion of culinary traditions from different corners, experimentation is an expression of culinary freedom. It allows individuals to redefine their relationship with food, transforming meals from mere sustenance into a sensory adventure.

One of the keys to successful flavor experimentation lies in understanding the basic principles of taste. Savory, sweet, sour, bitter, and umami—these fundamental tastes are the foundation upon which culinary experiments are built. When orchestrated thoughtfully, the interplay between these tastes creates symphonies on the palate. Encouraging readers to develop a nuanced appreciation for the subtleties of flavor is akin to teaching them the language of gastronomy, empowering them to articulate their culinary desires.

The world of spices and herbs emerges as a playground for those eager to experiment with flavors. Each spice is a tiny treasure chest, holding a universe of aromas and tastes within it. The art lies in combining them judiciously, elevating a dish from ordinary to extraordinary. Whether it's the warmth of cinnamon in a savory stew or the exotic allure of cardamom in a dessert, the judicious use of spices adds layers to the culinary experience, inviting readers to embark on a journey of sensory discovery.

Beyond spices, the world of unconventional pairings beckons adventurous palates. Experimenting with unexpected combinations, such as the fusion of sweet and savory or the juxtaposition of textures, introduces an element of surprise to the dining experience. It challenges preconceived notions about what works in harmony, urging readers to question culinary norms and paving the way to create entirely new flavor profiles.

Experimenting with flavors is not limited to haute cuisine; it extends to the humble domain of everyday meals. Encouraging readers to infuse creativity into their daily cooking rituals transforms routine into ritual. It's about turning a weeknight dinner into an occasion for exploration, transforming the act of nourishment into a celebration of taste. This approach to cooking fosters a sense of mindfulness, encouraging individuals to savor each bite and appreciate the nuances of the ingredients.

In the pursuit of culinary experimentation, the kitchen becomes a laboratory—a space where hypotheses are tested and the results are savored. Readers are invited to play the role of both scientist and artist, donning aprons as lab coats and wielding spatulas as creation instruments. Once a helpful space, the kitchen transforms into a realm of possibility, where the alchemy of cooking unfolds with each measured ingredient and every flicker of the flame.

As readers venture into the uncharted territory of flavor experimentation, they inevitably encounter failures alongside successes. The burnt edges, over-seasoned dishes, and culinary mishaps become badges of honor, proof of a courageous spirit unafraid of pushing boundaries. Encouraging readers to embrace these failures as valuable lessons is integral to culinary growth. It's a reminder that, in the kitchen, as in life, success often arises from a series of trial and error.

The spirit of experimentation extends beyond individual kitchens to the global culinary landscape. In an era where cultural exchange is commonplace, the fusion of diverse culinary traditions has become a hallmark of contemporary cooking. Encouraging readers to draw inspiration from different cultures to weave a tapestry of flavors that transcends geographical boundaries is an acknowledgment of the rich mosaic that defines our global food heritage.

Creating new traditions through flavor experimentation is a celebration of cultural diversity. It's an opportunity to pay homage to the culinary wisdom passed down through generations while infusing it with a contemporary twist. Readers are encouraged to explore the culinary traditions of their heritage, adapt them to modern tastes, and share these reinvented traditions with friends and family. In doing so, they contribute to the ever-evolving narrative of global cuisine.

Creating new culinary traditions is not a solitary endeavor but a communal celebration. Sharing recipes, exchanging cooking tips, and the collaborative effort of preparing a meal become acts of cultural preservation and evolution. In a seemingly fragmented world, breaking bread together becomes a unifying force, bridging gaps and fostering understanding.

Moreover, the encouragement to experiment with flavors and create new traditions is a call to embrace sustainability in the kitchen. As individuals explore plant-based alternatives, experiment with locally sourced ingredients, and minimize food waste, they contribute to a more environmentally conscious approach to cooking. Experimenting with flavors becomes a way of harmonizing culinary creativity with ecological responsibility, fostering a sense of connection to the earth and its resources.

In conclusion, encouraging readers to continue experimenting with flavors and creating new traditions is an invitation to embark on a journey of culinary self-discovery. It celebrates the boundless possibilities within the kitchen, waiting to be explored. Experimenting with flavors transcends the mere preparation of meals; it is a gateway to creativity, mindfulness, and a deeper connection to the rich tapestry of global cuisine. As readers embrace the joy of flavor exploration, they elevate their culinary skills and contribute to the ever-evolving story of food, weaving new traditions that enrich the shared experience of dining and celebration.

Wishing everyone a season filled with Peppermint Perfectio

In the tapestry of holiday traditions, few flavors weave the season's spirit as seamlessly as peppermint. As winter unfolds its frosty embrace, the aroma of peppermint dances through the air, conjuring images of crackling fires, twinkling lights, and the joyous laughter of loved ones. Wishing everyone a season filled with peppermint perfection is an invocation of the magic this humble herb imparts to our festivities. Beyond its role as a seasonal treat, peppermint transcends the boundaries of taste, offering a sensory journey that awakens memories, elevates moods, and becomes synonymous with the essence of the holidays.

With its refreshing fragrance and excellent, minty taste, Peppermint emerges as a culinary muse during the festive season. The ubiquitous candy canes that adorn trees and fill stockings are but a small testament to the widespread appeal of peppermint. Whether it graces hot cocoa with its aromatic essence or infuses cookies, cakes, and desserts with its refreshing flavor, peppermint becomes a culinary ambassador of holiday cheer. Wishing everyone a season filled with peppermint perfection is an acknowledgment of this versatile herb's role in transforming ordinary dishes into festive delights.

The allure of peppermint extends beyond its culinary contributions; it is a fragrance that evokes nostalgia and comfort. The mere scent of peppermint can transport individuals back to cherished moments of their past. Whether it's the memory of sipping peppermint tea by the fireplace or the delight of unwrapping a peppermint-infused gift, the aroma of this herb becomes a vessel for memories, intertwining with the fabric of our personal histories. Wishing everyone a season filled with peppermint perfection is an invitation to bask in the warmth of these recollections, creating new memories that will linger for years to come.

Moreover, the association of peppermint with the holiday season goes beyond the realm of taste and smell; it extends to the visual and tactile experience. The vibrant green hue of peppermint candies and the satisfying crunch as they break between teeth add layers to the multisensory celebration. Peppermint becomes a feast for the eyes, a symphony for the taste buds, and a tactile delight all wrapped into one. Wishing everyone a season filled with peppermint perfection acknowledges the holistic sensory experience that this herb bestows upon our festive celebrations.

Peppermint takes center stage in the world of beverages, offering a refreshing respite from the winter chill. With its aromatic steam rising from the cup, Peppermint tea becomes a soothing elixir that warms both body and soul. The infusion of peppermint into hot chocolate or coffee adds a layer of complexity, turning a simple drink into a decadent treat. Wishing everyone a season filled with peppermint perfection is a toast to the joy that a steaming mug of peppermint-infused goodness brings, fostering a sense of comfort and well-being.

Peppermint's therapeutic qualities also contribute to its seasonal significance. The refreshing aroma has long been associated with stress relief and mental clarity. As the holiday season unfolds with myriad demands and expectations, peppermint becomes a natural remedy, offering a moment of reprieve from the hustle and bustle. Wishing everyone a season filled with peppermint perfection is a wish for moments of calm amidst the festive frenzy. It is a reminder to savor the simple pleasures that peppermint, with its soothing properties, brings to our lives.

Incorporating peppermint into holiday decorations further cements its status as an emblem of the season. From peppermint-scented candles that fill homes with a comforting glow to peppermint-striped ornaments that adorn Christmas trees, this herb becomes a visual and olfactory motif of festive decor. Wishing everyone a season filled with peppermint perfection is an acknowledgment of this herb's role in creating an immersive and enchanting holiday ambiance. The visual symphony of red and white stripes and the refreshing scent transform spaces into winter wonderlands that captivate the senses.

Peppermint perfection extends to the realm of desserts, where this herb emerges as a star player in a symphony of sweet delights. Peppermint bark, with its layers of chocolate and mint, becomes a quintessential holiday treat that graces dessert tables and gift boxes. Peppermint-flavored cookies, cupcakes, and candies add a festive touch to homemade confections. Wishing everyone a season filled with peppermint perfection is an invitation to indulge in the decadence of these sweet creations, to savor the marriage of rich chocolate and cool mint that defines the holiday dessert landscape.

The iconic candy cane, with its red and white stripes and curved shepherd's crook shape, embodies the notion and tradition associated with peppermint. From hanging on Christmas trees to adorning gifts, the candy cane symbolizes sweetness and joy. Wishing everyone a season filled with peppermint perfection is a nod to the simple yet profound pleasure of unwrapping a candy cane, savoring its crisp texture, and allowing the minty sweetness to unfold on the palate. It is a celebration of the timeless appeal of this festive confection.

Beyond the confines of the kitchen and decorations, peppermint finds its way into personal care products during the holiday season. Peppermint-scented lotions, bath salts, and candles offer a spa-like experience that enhances the self-care aspect of the festivities. Wishing everyone a season filled with peppermint perfection extends beyond the culinary realm; it is an acknowledgment of this herb's holistic well-being, enveloping individuals in a cocoon of relaxation and rejuvenation during the holiday rush.

The cultural significance of peppermint in holiday traditions is not limited to a specific geographical region or religious affiliation. It transcends boundaries, becoming a global symbol of festive merriment. Wishing everyone a season filled with peppermint perfection is an inclusive sentiment, inviting individuals from diverse backgrounds to partake in this herb's joy. It is a recognition of the universal appeal of peppermint, which has found its way into the hearts and homes of people worldwide.

In conclusion, wishing everyone a season filled with peppermint perfection is more than a casual expression of goodwill. It is a recognition of peppermint's multi-faceted role in shaping the holiday experience. From its culinary contributions to its sensory allure, peppermint weaves a narrative of comfort, joy, and tradition. As individuals embark on the festive journey, the wish for peppermint perfection is a hope that the season unfolds with the sweet and refreshing magic that only this herb can bestow, creating moments that linger in the hearts and memories of all who partake in its delights.

Thank you for buying and reading/listening to our book. If you found this book useful/helpful please take a few minutes and leave a review on the platform where you purchased our book. Your feedback matters greatly to us.

Printed in the USA
CPSIA information can be obtained
at www.ICGtesting.com
LVHW022119200624
783564LV00013B/815